T0192157

Learn Pixi.js

Create Great Interactive Graphics for Games and the Web

Rex van der Spuy

Apress®

Learn Pixi.js

ISBN-13 (pbk): 978-1-4842-1095-6

ISBN-13 (electronic): 978-1-4842-1094-9

Managing Director: Welmoed Spahr
Lead Editor: Ben Renow-Clarke
Development Editor: Matthew Moodie
Technical Reviewer: Jason Sturges

Coordinating Editor: Jill Balzano
Copy Editor: Michael G. Laraque
Compositor: SPi Global
Indexer: SPi Global
Artist: SPi Global
Cover Designer: Anna Ishchenko

Distributed to the book trade worldwide by Springer Science+Business Media New York, 233 Spring Street, 6th Floor, New York, NY 10013. Phone 1-800-SPRINGER, fax (201) 348-4505, e-mail orders-ny@springer-sbm.com, or visit www.springer.com. Apress Media, LLC is a California LLC and the sole member (owner) is Springer Science+Business Media Finance Inc (SSBM Finance Inc). SSBM Finance Inc is a **Delaware** corporation.

For information on translations, please e-mail rights@apress.com, or visit www.apress.com.

Apress and friends of ED books may be purchased in bulk for academic, corporate, or promotional use. eBook versions and licenses are also available for most titles. For more information, reference our Special Bulk Sales–eBook Licensing web page at www.apress.com/bulk-sales.

Any source code or other supplementary material referenced by the author in this text is available to readers at www.apress.com. For detailed information about how to locate your book's source code, go to www.apress.com/source-code/.

For Freya, Queen of the Pixies!

Contents at a Glance

Contents

About the Author

Rex van der Spuy is a leading expert on video game design and interactive graphics and the author of the popular Foundation and Advanced series of books about how to make video games. Rex has designed games and performed interactive interface programming with Agency Interactive (Dallas), Scottish Power (Edinburgh), DC Interact (London), Draught Associates (London), and the Bank of Montreal (Canada). He's also built game engines and interactive interfaces for museum installations for PixelProject (Cape Town, South Africa), as well as "Ga," the world's smallest full-featured 2D game engine. He created and taught advanced courses in game design for many years at the Canadian School of India (Bangalore). The highlight of his career was programming video games on the Annapurna glacier at 4,500 meters (which, to his delight, was 1,000 meters higher than the maximum permissible operating altitude of his laptop).

About the Technical Reviewer

Jason Sturges is a cutting-edge technologist focused on ubiquitous delivery of immersive user experiences. Coming from a visualization background, he's always pushing the boundaries of computer graphics to the widest reach cross-platform, while maintaining natural and intuitive usability per device. From interactivity, motion, animations, and creative design, he has worked with numerous creative agencies on projects from kiosks to video walls to Microsoft Kinect games. Most recently, the core of his work has been mobile apps.

Committed to the open source community, he is also a frequent contributor to GitHub and Stack Overflow as a community resource, leveraging modern standards, solid design patterns, and best practices in multiple developer tool chains for Web, mobile, desktop, and other platforms.

Acknowledgments

Most illustrations and game characters for this book were created by the extraordinarily talented Kipp Lightburn (www.waymakercreative.com, waymakercreative@gmail.com). Thanks so much, Kipp!

The game graphics for Treasure Hunter were designed by Lanea Zimmerman and are from her brilliant Tiny 16 tileset (opengameart.org/content/tiny-16-basic).

For the game Pixie Perilousness! the green block graphic was designed by the author GameArtForge (opengameart.org/content/blocks-set-01).

Thanks to Chad Engler (github.com/englercj), one of Pixi's lead developers, for patiently and generously answering all of my technical questions in the Pixi discussion forum on html5gamedevs.com, and for single-handedly acting as Pixi's tireless one-man tech support team.

Thanks to Mat Groves (www.goodboydigital.com), the creator of Pixi..., for creating Pixi (!) and also for his enthusiastic support of this project and permission to use images and code samples from Pixi's web site. In particular, the sample code and image for the Rope object in Chapter 6 are based on Mat's original work.

The photograph of me was by taken by Sivan Ritter, in Arambol, Goa.

Introduction

If you want to start making games or applications for the Web, desktop, or mobile devices, Pixi is the best place to start. Pixi is an extremely fast 2D sprite rendering engine that helps you to display, animate, and manage interactive graphics, so that it's easy for you to make any visually rich interactive software you can imagine, using JavaScript and other HTML5 technologies. Pixi has a sensible, uncluttered API and includes many useful features, such as supporting texture atlases, and provides a streamlined system for animating sprites (interactive images).

Note What is an API? The acronym stands for "Application Programming Interface." The API refers to all of Pixi's objects and methods that let you make a bunch of cool stuff, without having to worry about how the underlying code actually works.

Pixi also gives you a complete **scene graph**, so that you can create hierarchies of nested sprites (sprites inside sprites), as well as letting you attach mouse and touch events directly to sprites. And, most important, Pixi gets out of your way, so that you can use as much or as little of it as you want, adapt it to your personal coding style, and integrate it seamlessly with other useful frameworks.

Pixi's API is actually a refinement of a well-worn and battle-tested API pioneered by Macromedia/Adobe Flash. Old-skool Flash developers will feel right at home. Other current sprite rendering frameworks use a similar API: CreateJS, Starling, Sparrow, and Apple's SpriteKit. The strength of Pixi's API is that it's general-purpose: it gives you total expressive freedom to make anything you like without dictating a specific workflow or architecture. That's good, because this means you can build your own architecture around it.

In this book, you'll learn everything you need to know to start using Pixi quickly. Although you can use Pixi to make any kind of interactive media, such as apps or web sites, I'm going to show you how to use it to make games. Why games? Because if you can make a game with Pixi, you can make anything else with Pixi. Besides, I like making games—and you will too!

But Pixi doesn't do everything! In this book, you're also going to learn to use a suite of easy-to-use helper libraries that extend Pixi's functionality in all kinds of exciting ways.

Bump: 2D collision functions

`github.com/kittykatattack/bump`

Charm: Tweening animation effects

`github.com/kittykatattack/charm`

Tink: Mouse and touch interactivity

`github.com/kittykatattack/tink`

Dust: Particle effects

`github.com/kittykatattack/dust`

SpriteUtilities: Advanced sprite creation utilities

`github.com/kittykatattack/spriteUtilities`

Sound.js: Music and sounds effects

`github.com/kittykatattack/sound.js`

It's everything you need to create anything you can imagine!

What Do You Have to Know?

To make use of this book, you should have a reasonable understanding of HTML and JavaScript. You don't have to be an expert or think of yourself as a "programmer." You're just an ambitious beginner with an eagerness to learn—just like I am!

If you don't know HTML and JavaScript, the best place to start learning is the book *Foundation Game Design with HTML5 and JavaScript*. I know for a fact that it's the best book, because I wrote it! It will give you all the coding and conceptual background you need to begin using this book. In fact, if you've read *Foundation Game Design*, then *Learn Pixi.js* is the perfect sequel.

This is not a tech-heavy book! It's a fun, practical book that gets to the point—fast. I'm not going to bog you down with mountains of heavy code or theory. I've kept the code simple and architecturally flat and expect that you're smart enough to be able to look at the examples and apply them to your own projects, in your own way. This book is just the map; it's up to you to take the journey.

Note If you're curious and want to take a deeper technical dive into video game programming, make sure to check out this book's hip and sophisticated older sister: *Advanced Game Design with HTML5 and JavaScript*. It shows how you can code a display engine similar to Pixi from scratch, as well as all the essential code you must know to make all kinds of 2D action games. It's a great complement to *Learn Pixi.js*, and you can share concepts and code between both books.

JavaScript ES6

This book is written in the latest version of JavaScript: ECMAScript 6, or ES6 for short. I'll introduce any new ES6 features in the code as you stumble upon them. You'll find them easy to learn. ES6 is really just a better, friendlier version of JavaScript that gets more done with less code. You won't look back once you start using it.

But, just to get you started, following are the two most important things you need to know about ES6.

1. Use let Instead of var

In most cases, you can declare a variable using the new keyword `let`.

```
let anyValue = 4;
```

In older versions of JavaScript (ES3 and ES5), you have to use `var`.

The `let` keyword gives the variable **block scope**. That means the variable can't be seen outside the pair of curly braces that it's defined in. Here's an example:

```
let say = "hello";
let outer = "An outer variable";

if (say === "hello") {
  let say = "goodbye";

  console.log(say);
  //Displays: "goodbye"

  console.log(outer);
  //Displays: "An outer variable"

  let inner = "An inner variable";
  console.log(inner);
  //Displays: "An inner variable"
}

console.log(say);
//Displays: "hello"

console.log(inner);
//Displays: ReferenceError: inner is not defined
```

A variable defined outside the `if` statement can be seen inside the `if` statement. But any variables defined inside the `if` statement can't be seen outside it. That's what block scope is. The `if` statement's curly braces define the block in which the variable is visible.

In this example, you can see that there are two variables called say. Because they were defined in different blocks, they're different variables. Changing the one inside the if statement doesn't change the one outside the if statement.

2. "Fat arrow" Function Expressions

ES6 has a new syntax for writing function expressions, as follows:

```
let saySomething = (value) => {
  console.log(value)
};
```

The => symbol represents an arrow pointing to the right, like this: ➔. It's visually saying "use the value in the parentheses to do some work in the next block of code that I'm pointing to."

You define function expressions in the same way you define a variable, by using let (or var). Each one also requires a semicolon after its closing brace. A function expression must be defined before you use it, like this:

```
let saySomething = (value) => {
  console.log(value)
};

saySomething("Hello from a function statement");
```

That's because function expressions are read at **runtime**. The code reads them in the same order, from top to bottom, that it reads the rest of the code. If you try to call a function expression before it has been defined, you'll get an error.

If you want to write a function that returns a value, use a return statement, such as the following:

```
let square = (x) => {
  return x * x;
};

console.log(square(4));
//Displays: 16
```

As a convenience, you can leave out the curly braces, the parentheses around parameters, and the return keyword, if your function is just one line of code with one parameter, as in the following:

```
let square = x => x * x;

console.log(square(4));
//Displays: 16
```

This is a neat, compact, and readable way to write functions.

Note A nice feature of arrow functions is that they make the scope inside a function the same as the scope outside it. This solves a big problem called **binding** that plagued earlier versions of JavaScript. Briefly, a whole class of quirks you had to work around are no longer issues. (For example, you no longer have to use the old `var self = this;` trick.)

You can write a function expression without using a fat arrow, as follows:

```
let saySomething = function(value) {
  console.log(value)
};
```

This will work the same way as the previous examples, with one important difference: the function's scope is local to that function, not the surrounding code. That means the value of "this" will be undefined. Here's an example that illustrates this difference:

```
let globalScope = () => console.log(this);

globalScope();
//Displays: Window...

let localScope = function(){
  console.log(this);
};

localScope();
//Displays: undefined
```

This difference is subtle but important. In most cases, I recommend that you use a fat arrow to create a function expression, because it's usually more convenient for code inside a function to share the same scope as the code outside the function. But in some rare situations, it's important to isolate the function's scope from the surrounding scope, and I'll introduce those situations when we encounter them.

Note This book was written when ES6 was brand new. So new, in fact, that no web browsers had yet fully implemented it. If you're in that same position, use an ES6 to ES5 transpiler such as Traceur or Babel to run the book's source code. In the book's source files, you'll find folders called ES5 that contain ES5 versions of all the source code and examples in this book.

Running a Web Server

To use Pixi, you'll also have to run a web server in your root project directory. The best way is to use node.js (`nodejs.org`) and then install the extremely easy-to-use http-server (`github.com/nodeapps/http-server`). However, you have to be comfortable working with the Unix command line, if you want to do that.

Note Are you afraid of the Unix command line? Don't be! Unix is a wonderfully retro-future way to scare your parents, and you can learn it in a few hours. Maybe start with the classic tutorial "Learn Unix in 10 minutes" (`freeengineer.org/learnUNIXin10minutes.html`) and follow it up with the "Unix Cheat Sheet" (`www.rain.org/~mkummel/unix.html`). Install a great little script called "Z" (`github.com/rupa/z`) to help you navigate the file system, and then start playing around. You'll also find dozens of videos on the Web for Unix for beginners, including Michael Johnston's excellent two-part series.

But if you don't want to mess around with the command line just yet, try the Mongoose web server (`cesanta.com/mongoose.shtml`) or just write all your code using one of the many HTML5-based text editors: Brackets, Light Table, or Atom. Any of these will launch a built-in web server for you automatically, when you run your code in a browser.

A Survival Guide for Future Pixi API Versions

This book was written when Pixi was in version 3, but Pixi is a fast-changing, living code library. What that means is that if you're using a future version of Pixi and run some code that isn't completely compatible with the code in this book, you'll have to use your judgment about how to adapt it to the new version. The good news is that Pixi's core user-facing API has been stable since version 1, so most of the code and techniques in this book should be relevant to future versions. But you'll have to stay on your toes! Following are some Future Pixi survival tips.

- **The object or method you're trying to use might have been renamed.** Pixi's development team sometimes likes to rearrange the furniture a bit, and they'll do so on a whim. That means they might change the names of some object or method names or give them new locations. For example, in version 2.0, the `TextureCache` object was located in `PIXI.TextureCache`, while in version 3.0, it was moved to `PIXI.utils.TextureCache`. Likewise, the `setFrame` method became the `frame` property. These aren't deal breakers. They're just cosmetic differences, and the code still works in the same way. But you'll have to be prepared to research possible future changes such as these and update your code if the JavaScript console gives you any errors or warnings.

- **Look for a deprecation document or script.** Pixi v3.0 has a file called `deprecation.js` that logs a message to the console if the code you're using has been changed from earlier versions. That's helpful, but you can't count on it being in future versions. If there's no `deprecation.js` file in the version of Pixi you're using, look for any document in Pixi's code repository that might list differences between versions. If you can't find one, post an issue in the code repository asking for help.
- **Use aliases for Pixi's objects and methods.** A way to slightly buffer yourself against a changing API is to create your own custom set of object and method names that just reference Pixi's. These are called **aliases**. For example, here's how you might create aliases for Pixi's `Sprite` class and `TextureCache` object:

```
let Sprite = PIXI.Sprite,
    TextureCache = PIXI.utils.TextureCache;
```

Do this right at the beginning of your program and then write the rest of your code using those aliases (`Sprite` and `TextureCache`) instead of Pixi's originals. This is helpful, because if Pixi's API changes, you only have to change what the alias is pointing to in one location, instead of every instance where you've used it throughout your entire program. Your own code base will be stable, even if Pixi's API fluctuates.

Note Another advantage to using aliases is that your code becomes more succinct: you don't have to prefix `PIXI` or `PIXI.utils` to everything. That can considerably shorten some complex lines of code and make your whole program more readable. For all these reasons, the sample code in this book uses aliases that follow this same format. You'll learn more about how to create and use aliases in Chapter 1.

Setting Up a Pixi Coding Environment

Let's find out how to set up a basic coding environment that you can use to run all the sample code in this book, as well as write your own original Pixi code. Do you have your web server running in your project's root directory, a text editor that you like to code in, and a web browser to run your code? Great, now you're ready to start working with Pixi!

Installing Pixi

Grab the latest version of the `pixi.min.js` file from Pixi's code repository (Pixi v3.0 was hosted at `github.com/pixijs/pixi.js`). You'll find the `pixi.min.js` file in the "bin" folder: `github.com/pixijs/pixi.js/tree/master/bin`. This one file is all you need to use Pixi. You can ignore all the other files in the repository; *you don't need them.*

Note If you prefer, you could alternatively use the un-minified `pixi.js` file. The minified file (`.min.js`) might run slightly faster, and it will certainly load faster. But the advantage to using the un-minified plain JS file is that if the compiler thinks there's a bug in Pixi's source code, it will give you an error message that displays the questionable code in a readable format. This is useful while you're working on a project, because even if the bug isn't actually in Pixi, the error might give you a hint as to what's wrong with your own code.

You can also use Git to install and use Pixi. (What is Git? If you don't know you can find out here: `github.com/kittykatattack/learningGit`.) Using Git has some advantages: you can just run `` `git pull` `` from the command line to update Pixi to the latest version. And, if you think you've found a bug in Pixi, you can fix it and submit a pull request to have the bug fix added to the main repository.

To clone the Pixi repository with Git, install `` `cd` `` into your project's root directory and type the following:

```
git clone git@github.com:pixijs/pixi.js.git
```

This automatically creates a folder called `pixi.js` and loads the latest version of Pixi into it.

Note You can also install Pixi using Node (`nodejs.org`) and Gulp (`gulpjs.com`), if you have to do a custom build of Pixi to include or exclude certain features. See Pixi's code repository for details on how to do this.

Create a Basic HTML Container Page

Next, create a basic HTML page and use a `<script>` tag to link the `pixi.min.js` file that you've just downloaded. The `<script>` tag's `src` property should be relative to your root directory on which your web server is running. Your `<script>` tag might look something like this:

```
<script src="pixi.min.js"></script>
```

Here's a basic HTML page that you could use to link Pixi and test that it's working:

```
<!doctype html>
<meta charset="utf-8">
<title>Hello World</title>
```

```
<body>
<script src="pixi.min.js"></script>
<script>

//Test that Pixi is working
console.log(PIXI);

</script>
</body>
```

This is the minimal amount of valid HTML you need to start creating projects with Pixi. If Pixi is linking correctly, `console.log(PIXI)` will display something such as this in your web browser's JavaScript console:

```
Object { VERSION: "3...
```

If you see that (or something similar) you know everything is working properly. Now you can start working with Pixi!

CHAPTER 1

Making Sprites

The basic building block for making things with Pixi is an object called a **sprite**. Sprites are just images that you can control with code. You can control their position, size, and a host of other properties that are useful for making interactive and animated graphics. Learning to make and control sprites is really the most important thing about learning to use Pixi. If you know how to make and display sprites, you're just a small step away from starting to make games or any other kind of interactive application.

In this chapter, you're going to learn everything you need in order to display and position sprites on Pixi's canvas, including the following:

- How to make a root container object called the **stage**
- How to make a **renderer**
- Using the `loader` to load images into Pixi's **texture cache**
- Making sprites from loaded images, including from **tilesets** and **texture atlases**

But before we can start making sprites, we have to create some sort of rectangular screen to display them on. Let's find out how to create one.

Creating the Renderer and Stage

Pixi has a `renderer` object that creates a display screen for you. It automatically generates an HTML `<canvas>` element and figures out how to display your images on the canvas. But you also have to create a special Pixi `Container` object called the `stage`. (Don't worry, you'll find out a little later in this chapter exactly what `Container` objects are and why you need them.) This `stage` object is going to be used as the root container that holds all the things you want Pixi to display. Here's the code you need to write to create a `renderer` and `stage`. Add this code to your HTML document between the `<script>` tags:

```
//Create the renderer
let renderer = PIXI.autoDetectRenderer(256, 256);

//Add the canvas to the HTML document
document.body.appendChild(renderer.view);
```

```
//Create a container object called the `stage`
let stage = new PIXI.Container();

//Tell the `renderer` to `render` the `stage`
renderer.render(stage);
```

This is the most basic code you need write to get started using Pixi. It produces a black 265 pixel by 256 pixel canvas element and adds it to your HTML document. Figure 1-1 shows what it looks like in a browser when you run this code.

Figure 1-1. *Pixi's renderer displays a black square in the browser*

This simple black square should fill your little programmer's heart with pure joy! That's because it's the first and most important step to begin displaying things with Pixi. Let's take a closer look at what all this code is doing.

Render Options

Pixi's `autoDetectRenderer` method figures out whether to use the Canvas Drawing API or WebGL to render graphics, depending on which is available.

```
let renderer = PIXI.autoDetectRenderer(256, 256);
```

Its first and second arguments are the width and height of the canvas. However, you can include an optional third argument with some additional values you can set. This third argument is an object literal, and here's how you could use it to set the renderer's anti-aliasing, transparency, and resolution:

```
renderer = PIXI.autoDetectRenderer(
  256, 256,
  {antialias: false, transparent: false, resolution: 1}
);
```

This third argument (the object highlighted in the preceding) is optional. If you're happy with Pixi's default settings, you can leave it out; there's usually no need to change them. But what do those options do? The `antialias` option smooths the edges of fonts and graphic primitives. (WebGL anti-aliasing isn't available on all platforms, so you'll have to test this on your application's target platform.) The `transparent` option makes the canvas background transparent. The `resolution` option makes it easier to work with displays of varying resolutions and pixel densities. Usually, just keep resolution at 1 for most projects, and you'll be fine. But take a look at Chapter 6 for more information about working with different resolutions.

■ **Note** The renderer has an additional, fourth, option called `preserveDrawingBuffer` that defaults to `false`. The only reason to set it to `true` is if you ever have to call Pixi's specialized `dataToURL` method in a WebGL canvas context. You might have to do this if you ever want to convert a Pixi canvas to an HTML image object.

Pixi's `autoDetectRenderer` will decide whether to use the Canvas Drawing API or WebGL to display images. It defaults to WebGL, which is good, because WebGL is incredibly fast and lets you use some spectacular visual effects that you'll learn all about in this book. But if you have to force Canvas Drawing API rendering over WebGL, you can do it like this:

```
renderer = new PIXI.CanvasRenderer(256, 256);
```

Only the first two arguments are required: width and height.

You can also force WebGL rendering like this:

```
renderer = new PIXI.WebGLRenderer(256, 256);
```

Now let's find out how to improve the appearance of the renderer.

Customizing the Canvas

The `renderer.view` object is just a plain old ordinary `<canvas>` object, so you can control it the same way you would control any other canvas object. Here's how to give the canvas an optional dashed border:

```
renderer.view.style.border = "1px dashed black";
```

If you have to change the background color of the canvas after you've created it, set the renderer object's `backgroundColor` property to any hexadecimal color value. Here's how you could set it to pure white:

```
renderer.backgroundColor = 0xFFFFFF;
```

■ **Note** A web search will turn up many hexadecimal color charts that you can use to select an appropriate background color.

If you want to find the width or the height of the renderer, use `renderer.view.width` and `renderer.view.height`.

To change the size of the canvas, use the renderer's `resize` method, and supply any new width and height values, as follows:

```
renderer.resize(512, 512);
```

If you want to make the canvas fill the entire window, you can apply this CSS styling:

```
renderer.view.style.position = "absolute";
renderer.view.style.width = window.innerWidth + "px";
renderer.view.style.height = window.innerHeight + "px";
renderer.view.style.display = "block";
```

But, if you do that, make sure you also set the default padding and margins to 0 on all your HTML elements with this bit of CSS code:

```
<style>* {padding: 0; margin: 0}</style>
```

(The asterisk, *, in the preceding code, is the CSS "universal selector," which just means "all the tags.") Without this bit of CSS, you might notice a few pixels of default padding between the edge of the browser and Pixi's canvas.

Scaling the Canvas to the Browser Window

You can use a custom function called `scaleToWindow()`to scale Pixi's canvas to the maximum size of the browser's window. (You'll find `scaleToWindow` in the library folder of this book's source code, or `scaleToWindow`'s own source code repository: `github.com/kittykatattack/scaleToWindow`.) `scaleToWindow` will also align the canvas for the best vertical or horizontal fit inside the browser window. For example, if you have a canvas that's wider than it is tall, it will be centered vertically inside the browser. If the canvas is taller than it is wide, it will be centered horizontally. Figure 1-2 show an example of these two alignments.

Figure 1-2. *Use the custom `scaleToWindow` function to scale and align the canvas inside the browser window*

Here's how to use `scaleToWindow` to scale and align Pixi's canvas:

```
scaleToWindow(renderer.view, borderColor);
```

The optional second argument lets you set the color of the browser's background that borders the canvas. You can supply any RGB, HSLA, or hexadecimal color value, as well as the any HTML color string, such as "blue" or "red." (If you don't supply this optional color, the border will be set to a neutral dark gray: #2C3539.)

The `scaleToWindow` function also returns the scale value that the canvas is scaled to. You can find the scale value like this:

```
let scale = scaleToWindow(renderer.view);
```

This will give you a number, possibly like 1.98046875, that tells you the ratio by which the canvas was scaled. This might be an important value to know if you ever have to convert browser pixel coordinates to the scaled pixel values of the canvas. For example, if you have a pointer object that tracks the mouse's position in the browser, you might have to convert those pixel positions to the scaled canvas coordinates, to find out if the mouse is touching something inside the canvas. Some general code such as the following will do the trick:

```
pointer.x = pointer.x / scale;
pointer.y = pointer.y / scale;
```

■ **Note** You'll learn about how to create and use a Pixi pointer in Chapter 7.

Optionally, you might also want the canvas to rescale itself every time the size of the browser window is changed. If that's the case, call `scaleToWindow` inside a `window` event listener, as follows:

```
window.addEventListener("resize", event => {
  scaleToWindow(renderer.view);
});
```

Now that you know how to create a Pixi canvas, let's find out how to display images on it.

Pixi Sprites

In the previous section, you learned how to create a `stage` object, like this:

```
let stage = new PIXI.Container();
```

But what is the stage? It's a Pixi `Container` object. You can think of a container as a kind of empty box that will group together and store whatever you put inside it. The `stage` object that we created is the root container for all the visible things in your scene. Pixi requires that you have one root container object, because the renderer needs something to render.

```
renderer.render(stage);
```

Whatever you put inside the `stage` will be rendered on the canvas. Right now, the `stage` is empty, but soon we're going to start putting things inside it.

■ **Note** You can give your root container any name you like. Call it *scene* or *root*, if you prefer. The name *stage* is just an old but useful convention, and one I'll be sticking to in this book.

So what do you put on the stage? Special image objects that you can control with code, called **sprites**. Pixi has a specialized `Sprite` **class** that is a versatile way to make game sprites. (In JavaScript, a class is a function that creates and returns an object with useful properties that you can access or change.) The `Sprite` class gives you three main ways to create sprites, as follows:

1. From a single image file.
2. From a sub-image on a **tileset**. A tileset is a single, big image that includes all the images you'll require in your game or application.
3. From a **texture atlas** (a JSON file that defines the size and position of an image on a tileset).

You're going to learn all three ways to make sprites, using Pixi's `Sprite` class, but before you do, let's find out what you need to know about images before you can display them with Pixi.

Understanding Textures and the Texture Cache

Pixi renders images using the GPU (Graphics Processing Unit) of the system that Pixi is running on: a computer, mobile phone, or tablet. The GPU is just a specialized chip for displaying high-performance graphics. The web browser communicates with the GPU, using an HTML5 API called WebGL. So, to display your image, it has to be in a format that WebGL can easily communicate to the GPU.

A WebGL-ready image is called a **texture**. Before you can make a sprite display an image, you have to convert an ordinary image file into a WebGL texture. To keep everything working fast and efficiently under the hood, Pixi uses a **texture cache** to store and reference all the textures your sprites will need. The names of the textures are strings that match the file locations of the images they refer to. That means that if you have a texture that was loaded from `"images/anyImage.png"`, you could find it in the texture cache like this:

```
PIXI.utils.TextureCache["images/anyImage.png"];
```

The textures are stored in a WebGL compatible format that's efficient for Pixi's renderer to work with. You can then use Pixi's `Sprite` class to make a new sprite, using the texture. Here's how:

```
let texture = PIXI.utils.TextureCache["images/anyImage.png"];
let sprite = new PIXI.Sprite(texture);
```

■ **Note** You can always spot a class because the first letter of the class is capitalized (like the *S* in `Sprite`.) Also, classes are always instantiated by using the `new` keyword. (**Instantiate** means to make a new copy of something, the same way you might make a new cookie from a cookie cutter.) `Sprite`, `Container`, and `TextureCache` are examples of Pixi classes that you've seen so far. Some classes, such as `TextureClass`, can be used directly without having to be instantiated. That's because you don't need more than one copy; you just work directly with the single existing class. Classes that you use directly without instantiating are sometimes referred to as **static classes**.

But how do you load the image file and convert it into a texture? Use Pixi's built-in `loader` object.

Loading Images

Pixi's powerful loader object is all you need to load any kind of image. Here's how to use it to load an image and call a function called setup when the image has finished loading.

```
PIXI.loader
  .add("image.png")
  .load(setup);

function setup() {
  //This code will run when the loader has finished loading the image
}
```

Pixi's development team recommends that if you use the loader, you should create the sprite by referencing the texture in the loader's resources object, like this:

```
let sprite = new PIXI.Sprite(PIXI.loader.resources("image.png").texture);
```

Here's an example of some complete code you could write to load an image, call the setup function, and create the sprite from the loaded image:

```
PIXI.loader
  .add("image.png")
  .load(setup);

function setup() {
  let sprite = new PIXI.Sprite(PIXI.loader.resources("image.png").texture);
}
```

This is the general format we'll be using to load images and create sprites in this book.

You can load multiple images at a single time by listing them with chainable add methods, like this:

```
PIXI.loader
  .add("imageOne.png")
  .add("imageTwo.png")
  .add("imageThree.png")
  .load(setup);
```

■ **Note** In JavaScript, chainable methods are methods, separated by dots, that you can run in sequence: `anyObject.firstMethod().secondMethod().thirdMethod();`. You can make your own chainable methods by setting the method's return value to the parent object that it belongs to. JavaScript developers discovered almost by accident that you could do this, and it can be a very readable way to eliminate monotonous blocks of repetitive code.

Better yet, just list all the files you want to load in an array inside a single add method, like this:

```
PIXI.loader
  .add([
    "images/imageOne.png",
    "images/imageTwo.png",
    "images/imageThree.png"
  ])
  .load(setup);
```

Pixi's `loader` also lets you load JSON files, which you'll learn all about ahead.

■ **Note** Pixi's `Sprite` class also has a method called `fromImage` that lets you make a sprite directly from an image file, like this:

```
let sprite = PIXI.Sprite.fromImage("image.png");
```

If `Sprite.fromImage` detects that the image you're trying to load isn't already in Pixi's texture cache, it will helpfully try and load it for you automatically, without you having to use the `loader`. However, I suggest you don't use this feature and always preload a texture with Pixi's `loader`. That's so you have a guarantee that the texture truly has loaded. If you write some code that tries to access a texture that hasn't fully loaded, you could encounter all kinds of strange errors. Pixi's `Texture` class also has a `fromImage` method that works in the same way.

Displaying Sprites

After you've loaded an image and used it to make a sprite, there are two more things you have to do before you can actually see it on Pixi's canvas.

1. You have to add the sprite to Pixi's `stage` with the `stage.addChild` method, like this:

   ```
   stage.addChild(anySprite);
   ```

The `stage` is the main container that holds all of your sprites.

2. You have to tell Pixi's `renderer` to render the `stage`.

   ```
   renderer.render(stage);
   ```

Remember: *None of your sprites will be visible before you do these two things.*

Before we continue, let's look at a practical example of how to use what you've just learned to display a single image. In this chapter's source code folder, you'll find a 96 by 48 pixel PNG image of a game character (see Figure 1-3). In keeping with the theme, it's of a pixie!

Figure 1-3. *An image of a game character*

Here's the JavaScript code to load the image, create a sprite, and display it on Pixi's stage:

```
//Create the stage and renderer
let stage = new PIXI.Container(),
    renderer = PIXI.autoDetectRenderer(256, 256);
document.body.appendChild(renderer.view);

//Use Pixi's built-in `loader` object to load an image
PIXI.loader
  .add("images/pixie96x48.png")
  .load(setup);

//This `setup` function will run when the image has loaded
function setup() {

  //Create the sprite from the texture
  let pixie = new PIXI.Sprite(
    PIXI.loader.resources["images/pixie96x48.png"].texture
  );

  //Add the sprite to the stage
  stage.addChild(pixie);

  //Render the stage
  renderer.render(stage);
}
```

When this code runs, here's what you'll see (Figure 1-4):

Figure 1-4. *Displaying a sprite on the stage*

Now we're getting somewhere!

Removing Sprites

If you ever have to remove a sprite from the stage, use the `removeChild` method:

```
stage.removeChild(anySprite);
```

But, usually, setting a sprite's `visible` property to `false` will be a simpler and more efficient way of making sprites disappear.

```
anySprite.visible = false;
```

Pixi sprites also have a special method called `destroy`, which is used to manually clear out GPU memory. Use `destroy` like this:

```
anySprite.destroy(true, true);
```

The two Boolean arguments are optional, but you should set them both to `true`. They refer to the sprite's texture and its base texture. (You'll learn more about the base texture ahead.) The only time you'll ever have to use `destroy` is in extreme cases in which your game is creating and destroying a lot of sprites, and you notice unusually high GPU memory usage. In normal day-to-day Pixi programming, you'll probably never have to use `destroy`.

■ **Note** Pixi textures also have a `destroy` method. If you ever have to, you can manually clear the entire texture cache of GPU memory with the following bit of code:

```
Object.keys(PIXI.utils.TextureCache).forEach(texture => {
 PIXI.utils.TextureCache[texture].destroy(true);
});.
```

But be careful: never destroy a sprite or texture if it's used somewhere else in your code.

Using Aliases

You can save yourself a little typing and make your code more readable by creating short-form aliases for the Pixi objects and methods that you use frequently. For example, is `PIXI.utils.TextureCache` too much to type? I think so, especially in a big project in which you might use it dozens of times. So, create a shorter alias that points to it, like this:

```
let TextureCache = PIXI.utils.TextureCache;
```

Then, use that alias in place of the original, like this:

```
let texture = TextureCache["images/cat.png"];
```

In addition to letting you write more succinct code, using aliases has an extra benefit: it helps to buffer you slightly from Pixi's frequently changing API. If Pixi's API changes in future versions—which it will!—you'll only have to update these aliases to Pixi objects and methods in one place, at the beginning of your program, instead of in every instance in which they're used throughout your code.

To see how to set up and use aliases, let's rewrite the code we wrote to load an image and display it, using aliases for all the Pixi objects and methods.

```
//Aliases
let Container = PIXI.Container,
    autoDetectRenderer = PIXI.autoDetectRenderer,
    loader = PIXI.loader,
    resources = PIXI.loader.resources,
    Sprite = PIXI.Sprite;

//Create the stage and renderer
let stage = new Container(),
    renderer = autoDetectRenderer(256, 256);
document.body.appendChild(renderer.view);
```

```
//Load an image and call the `setup` function
loader
  .add("images/pixie96x48.png")
  .load(setup);

function setup() {

  //Create the sprite, add it to the stage and render it
  let pixie = new Sprite(resources["images/pixie96x48.png"].texture);
  stage.addChild(pixie);
  renderer.render(stage);
}
```

Most of the examples in this book will use aliases for Pixi objects that follow this same model. Unless otherwise stated, you can assume that all the code examples use aliases.

This is all you need to know to start loading images and creating sprites with Pixi.

A Little More About Loading Things

The format I've shown you above is what I suggest you use as your standard template for loading images and displaying sprites. So, you can safely ignore the next few paragraphs and jump straight to the next section, "Positioning Sprites." But Pixi's `loader` object is quite sophisticated and includes a few features that you should be aware of, even if you don't use them on a regular basis. Let's look at some of the most useful.

Making a Sprite from an Ordinary HTML Image Object or Canvas

For optimization and efficiency, it's always best to make a sprite from a texture that's been preloaded into Pixi's texture cache. But if for some reason you have to make a texture from a regular HTML image object, you can do so using Pixi's `BaseTexture` (`PIXI.BaseTexture`) and `Texture` (`PIXI.Texture`) classes.

```
let base = new BaseTexture(anyImageObject),
    texture = new Texture(base),
    sprite = new Sprite(texture);
```

You can use `BaseTexture.fromCanvas` if you want to make a texture from any existing canvas element:

```
let base = BaseTexture.fromCanvas(anyCanvasElement);
```

If you want to change the texture the sprite is displaying, use the sprite's texture property. Set it to any Texture object, like this:

```
anySprite.texture = TextureCache["anyTexture.png"];
```

You can use this technique to interactively change the sprite's appearance if something significant happens to it in the game. (Although, as you'll see ahead, there's a better way to do this using **frames**.)

Assigning a Name to a Loading File

It's possible to assign a unique name to each resource you want to load. Just supply the name (a string) as the first argument in the loader's add method. For example, here's how to name an image of a cat as catImage:

```
loader
  .add("catImage", "images/cat.png")
  .load(setup);
```

This creates an object called catImage in loader.resources. And that means you can create a sprite by referencing the catImage object, like this:

```
let cat = new Sprite(loader.resources.catImage.texture);
```

However, I recommend you don't use this feature! That's because you'll have to remember all the names you've given each loaded file, as well as make sure you don't accidentally use the same name more than once. Using the file path name, as we've done in previous examples, is simpler and less error-prone. But, just in case you can think of a clever use for this that I haven't, now you know!

Monitoring Load Progress

Pixi's loader has a special progress event that can call a customizable callback function each time a file loads. progress events are called by the loader's on method, like this:

```
loader.on("progress", loadProgressHandler);
```

Here's how to include the on method in the loading chain and call a user-definable function called loadProgressHandler each time a file loads:

```
loader
  .add([
    "images/one.png",
    "images/two.png",
    "images/three.png"
  ])
  .on("progress", loadProgressHandler)
  .load(setup);
```

```
function loadProgressHandler() {
  console.log("loading");
}

function setup() {
  console.log("setup");
}
```

Each time one of the files loads, the `progress` event calls `loadProgressHandler` to display "loading" in the console. When all three files have loaded, the `setup` function will run. Here's the output of the preceding code in the console:

```
loading
loading
loading
setup
```

That's neat, but it gets better. You can also find out exactly which file has loaded and what percentage of overall files have currently loaded. You can do this by adding optional `loader` and `resource` parameters to the `loadProgressHandler`, like this:

```
function loadProgressHandler(loader, resource) { //...
```

You can then use `resource.url` to find the file that's currently loaded. (Use `resource.name`, if you want to find the optional name that you might have assigned to the file, as the first argument in the add method.) And you can use `loader.progress` to find what percentage of total resources have currently loaded. Here's some code that does just that:

```
PIXI.loader
  .add([
    "images/one.png",
    "images/two.png",
    "images/three.png"
  ])
  .on("progress", loadProgressHandler)
  .load(setup);

function loadProgressHandler(loader, resource) {

  //Display the file `url` currently being loaded
  console.log(`loading: ${resource.url}`);

  //Display the percentage of files currently loaded
  console.log(`progress: ${loader.progress}`);
}
```

```
function setup() {
  console.log("All files loaded");
}
```

Here's what this code will display in the console when it runs:

```
loading: images/one.png
progress: 33.333333333333336%
loading: images/two.png
progress: 66.66666666666667%
loading: images/three.png
progress: 100%
All files loaded
```

That's really cool, because you could use this as the basis for creating a loading progress bar. This code also demonstrates a JavaScript ES6 feature called a template string.

```
`loading: ${resource.url}`
```

It's a way to create a new string by combining an existing string (`` `loading` ``) with a variable (`resource.url`). (Note that template strings are surrounded by **backtick characters**, not single quotes. You'll probably find the backtick character near the top left of your keyboard, possibly sharing the same key as the tilde [~] character.) The template string above is the equivalent of writing the following older JavaScript code:

```
"loading:" + resource.url
```

There are additional properties you can access on the resource object. `resource.error` will tell you of any possible error that occurred while trying to load a file. `resource.data` lets you access the file's raw binary data. For more information, visit Pixi's `loader` code repository: `github.com/englercj/resource-loader`.

More About Pixi's Loader

Pixi's `loader` is ridiculously feature-rich and configurable. Let's take a quick bird's-eye view of its usage, to get you started.

The `loader`'s chainable `add` method takes four basic arguments:

```
add(name, url, optionObject, callbackFunction)
```

Here's what the `loader`'s source code documentation has to say about these parameters:

> `name` (string): The name of the resource to load. If it's not passed, the `url` is used.
>
> `url` (string): The URL for this resource, relative to the `baseUrl` of the `loader`

`options` (object literal): The options for the `loader`

`options.crossOrigin` (Boolean): Is the request cross-origin? The default is to determine automatically.

`options.loadType`: How should the resource be loaded? The default value is `Resource.LOAD_TYPE.XHR`.

`options.xhrType`: How should the data being loaded be interpreted when using XHR? The default value is `Resource.XHR_RESPONSE_TYPE.DEFAULT`.

`callbackFunction`: The function to call when this specific resource completes loading.

The only one of these arguments that's required is the `url` (the file that you want to load). You won't typically have to change or set any of these options, but, just in case, you now know how to access them if you do.

Here are examples of some ways you could use the add method to load files. This first are what the docs call the `loader`'s "normal syntax":

```
.add("key", "http://...", () => {})
.add("http://...", () => {})
.add("http://...")
```

And these are examples of the `loader`'s "object syntax":

```
.add({
  name: "key2",
  url: "http://..."
}, () => {})

.add({
  url: "http://..."
}, () => {})

.add({
  name: "key3",
  url: "http://...",
  onComplete: () => {}
})

.add({
  url: "https://...",
  onComplete: () => {},
  crossOrigin: true
})
```

You can also pass the add method an array of objects, or URLs, or both:

```
.add([
  {name: "key4", url: "http://...", onComplete: () => {} },
  {url: "http://...", onComplete: () => {} },
  "http://..."
])
```

■ **Note** If you ever have to reset the `loader` to load a new batch of files, call the `loader`'s `reset` method: `PIXI.loader.reset();`.

Pixi's `loader` has many more advanced features, including options to let you load and parse binary files of all types. This is not something you'll have to do on a day-to-day basis and is outside the scope of this book, so for more information, make sure to check out the `loader`'s source code repository at `github.com/englercj/resource-loader`.

Positioning Sprites

Now that you know how to create and display sprites, let's find out how to position and resize them.

X and Y Properties

You can change the position of any sprite by setting its x and y properties. The x property refers to how far, in pixels, the sprite's top left corner is from the left side of the canvas. The y property refers to how far the sprite's top left corner is from the top of the canvas. x values start at 0, at the left side of the canvas, and increase as the sprite moves right. y values start at 0, the top of the canvas, and increase as the sprite moves down.

A practical example will make this clear. Imagine that you've got a Pixi canvas with a width and height of 256. You have a sprite called `cat` that you want to position 96 pixels to the right of the canvas and 128 pixels below the top of the canvas. You can position the sprite using its x and y properties, like this:

```
cat.x = 96;
cat.y = 128;
```

Figure 1-5 illustrates this.

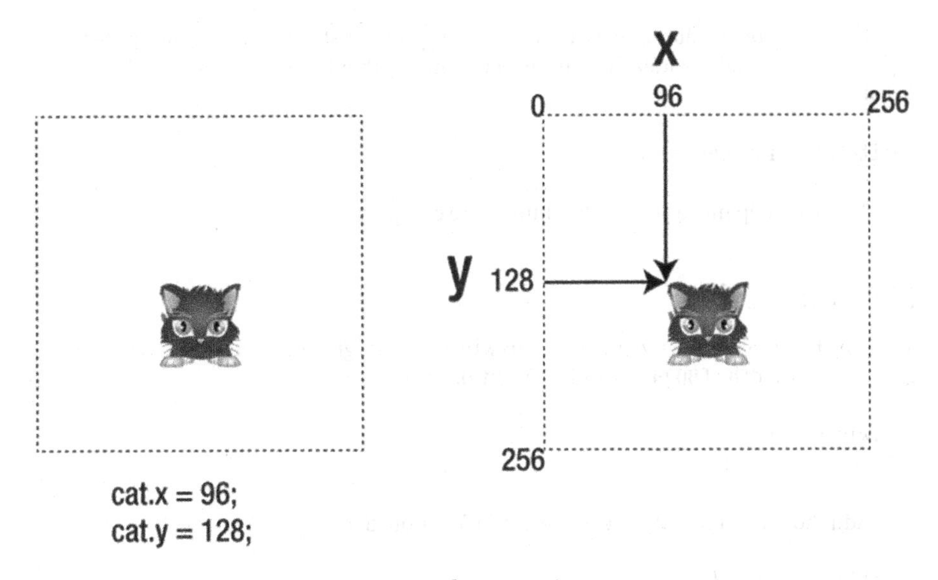

Figure 1-5. *Positioning a sprite using x and y properties*

You can add those two lines of code anywhere inside the setup function, after you've created the sprite. Here's where to put them in the context of the entire setup function.

```
function setup() {

  //Create the `cat` sprite
  let cat = new Sprite(resources["images/cat64x64.png"].texture);

  //Change the sprite's position
  cat.x = 96;
  cat.y = 128;

  //Add the cat to the stage so you can see it
  stage.addChild(cat);

  //Render the stage
  renderer.render(stage);
}
```

These two new lines of code will move the cat 96 pixels to the right and 128 pixels down, just as you can see in Figure 1-5.

The cat's top left corner (its left ear) represents its x and y anchor point. To make the cat move to the right, increase the value of its x property. To make the cat move down, increase the value of its y property. If the cat has an x value of 0, it will be at the very left side of the canvas. If it has a y value of 0, it will be at the very top of the canvas.

Pixi gives you an alternative way to position sprites. Instead of setting the sprite's x and y properties independently, you can set them together in a single line of code, like this:

```
sprite.position.set(x, y);
```

That can help make your code a little more compact.

Size and Scale

You can change a sprite's size by setting its `width` and `height` properties. Here's how to give the cat a `width` of 80 pixels and a `height` of 120 pixels:

```
cat.width = 80;
cat.height = 120;
```

Add those two lines of code to the `setup` function, like this:

```
function setup() {

  //Create the `cat` sprite
  let cat = new Sprite(resources["images/cat64x64.png"].texture);

  //Change the sprite's position
  cat.x = 96;
  cat.y = 128;

  //Change the sprite's size
  cat.width = 80;
  cat.height = 120;

  //Add the cat to the stage
  stage.addChild(cat);
}
```

Figure 1-6 shows the result.

Figure 1-6. *Changing a sprite's width and height*

You can see that the cat's position (its top left corner) didn't change, only its width and height. Sprites also have `scale.x` and `scale.y` properties that change the sprite's width and height proportionately. Here's how to set the cat's scale to half size:

```
cat.scale.x = 0.5;
cat.scale.y = 0.5;
```

`scale` values are numbers between 0 and 1 that represent a percentage of the sprite's size. 1 means 100% (full size), while 0.5 means 50% (half size).

■ **Note** Values between 0 and 1 are very commonly used in computer graphics and often referred to as **normalized values**.

You can double the sprite's size by setting its `scale` values to 2, like this:

```
cat.scale.x = 2;
cat.scale.y = 2;
```

Pixi has an alternative, concise way for you to set the sprite's scale in one line of code, using the `scale.set` method.

```
cat.scale.set(0.5, 0.5);
```

If that appeals to you, use it!

Rotation

You can make a sprite rotate by setting its `rotation` property to a value in radians.

```
cat.rotation = 0.5;
```

■ **Note** Radians are units of measurement for circles that are a bit easier to work with, mathematically, than degrees. One radian is the measurement you get when you take a circle's radius and wrap it around the edge of the circle. 3.14 radians equal half a circle, which, very conveniently, equals pi (3.14). A full circle is 6.28 radians (pi * 2). There are about 57.3 degrees in one radian, and if you ever have to convert degrees to radians, or radians to degrees, use the following formulas:

```
radians = degrees * (Math.PI / 180);
degrees = radians * (180 / Math.PI);
```

But around which point does that rotation occur? You've seen that a sprite's top left corner represents its x and y position. That point is called the **anchor point**. If you set the sprite's `rotation` property to something like 0.5, the rotation will occur *around the sprite's anchor point.* Figure 1-7 illustrates this.

cat.rotation = 0.5;

Figure 1-7. *Rotation occurs around the sprite's anchor point*

You can see that the anchor point, the cat's left ear, is the center of the imaginary circle around which the cat is rotating. What if you want the sprite to rotate around its center? Change the sprite's anchor point, so that it's centered inside the sprite, like this:

```
cat.anchor.x = 0.5;
cat.anchor.y = 0.5;
```

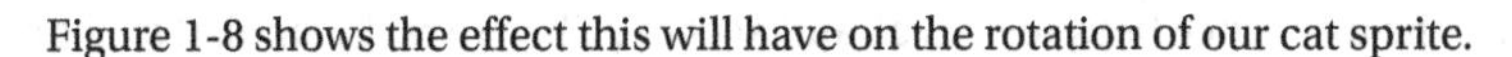

Figure 1-8 shows the effect this will have on the rotation of our cat sprite.

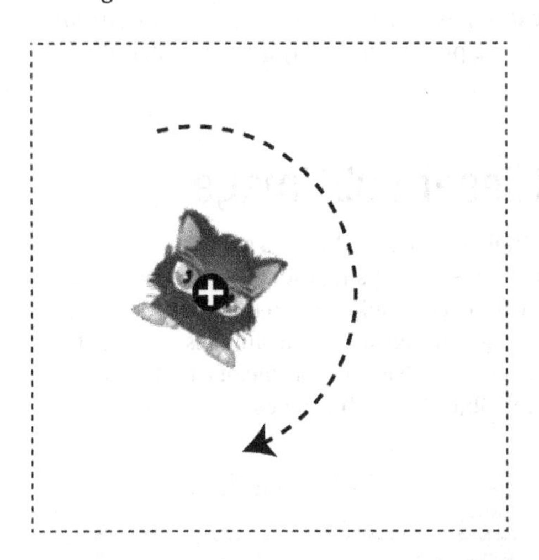

```
cat.anchor.x = 0.5;
cat.anchor.y = 0.5;
cat.rotation = 0.5;
```

Figure 1-8. *Set the sprite's anchor to change the point around which it rotates*

The `anchor.x` and `anchor.y` values represent a percentage of the sprite's image texture dimensions, from 0 to 1 (0% to 100%). Setting it to 0.5 (50%) centers the texture over the point.

The location of the point itself won't change, only the way the texture is positioned over it. You can also see in Figure 1-8 that the sprite's texture shifts up and to the left. This is an important side effect to remember!

Just like with `position` and `scale`, you can set the anchor's x and y values with one line of code, like this:

```
sprite.anchor.set(x, y);
```

Sprites also have a `pivot` property, which works in a similar way to `anchor.` `pivot` sets the position of the sprite's x/y origin point. Usually, the x/y origin point is the sprite's top left corner, but `pivot` lets you change that. If you reposition the `pivot` point and then rotate the sprite, the sprite will rotate around that new origin point. For example, the following code will set the sprite's `pivot.x` point to 32 and its `pivot.y` point to 32:

```
cat.pivot.set(32, 32);
```

This shifts the sprite's x/y origin point 32 pixels to the right and 32 pixels down from its top left corner. Assuming that the sprite is 64 by 64 pixels, the sprite will now rotate around its center point. Its x/y origin point will now also be the sprite's center, not its top left corner. The visual effect of this code is identical to what occurred when we changed the anchor point in Figure 1-8.

So what's the difference between `pivot` and `anchor`? They're really similar! `anchor` shifts the origin point of the sprite's image texture, using a 0 to 1 normalized value. `pivot` shifts the origin of the sprite's `x` and `y` point, using pixel values. Play around with both `anchor` and `pivot` and see which you prefer!

Making a Sprite from a Tileset Sub-image

You now know how to make a sprite from a single image file. But, as a game or interactive designer, you'll usually be making your sprites using **tilesets** (also known as **spritesheets**). Pixi has some convenient built-in ways to help you do this.

A tileset is a single image file that contains sub-images. The sub-images represent all the graphics you want to use in your game. Figure 1-9 is an example of a typical tileset image that contains game characters and game objects as sub-images.

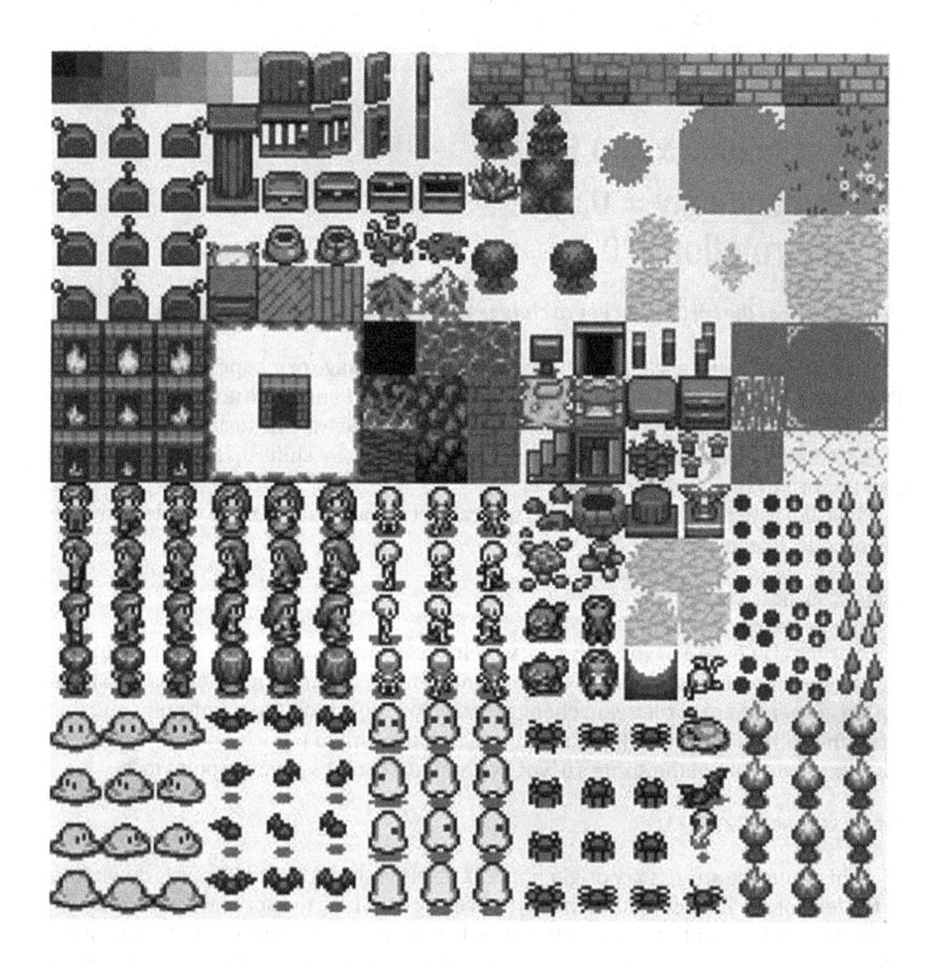

Figure 1-9. *A tileset is a single image that contains sub-images*

The entire tileset is 512 by 512 pixels. Each image is in its own 32-by-32-pixel grid cell. Storing and accessing all your game graphics on a tileset is a very processor- and memory-efficient way to work with graphics, and Pixi is optimized for them.

You can capture a sub-image from a tileset by defining a rectangular area that's the same size and position as the sub-image you want to extract. Imagine that you want to extract the image of the girl adventurer character that you can see near the center of the tileset. Let's look at code that will do this.

First, load the `tileset.png` image with Pixi's `loader`, just as you've done in earlier examples.

```
loader
  .add("images/tileset.png")
  .load(setup);
```

Next, when the image has loaded, use a rectangular subsection of the tileset to create the sprite's image. Here's the code that extracts the sub-image, creates the `adventuress` character sprite, and positions and displays her on Pixi's canvas:

```
function setup() {

  //Create the `tileset` sprite from the texture
  let texture = TextureCache["images/tileset.png"];

  //Create a rectangle object that defines the position and
  //size of the sub-image you want to extract from the texture
  let rectangle = new Rectangle(160, 256, 32, 32);

  //Tell the texture to use that rectangular section
  texture.frame = rectangle;

  //Create the sprite from the texture
  let adventuress = new Sprite(texture);

  //Position the sprite on the canvas
  adventuress.x = 64;
  adventuress.y = 64;

  //Scale the sprite up so it's 3 times bigger than the original image
  adventuress.scale.set(3, 3);

  //Add the sprite to the stage
  stage.addChild(adventuress);

  //Render the stage
  renderer.render(stage);
}
```

Figure 1-10 shows the result. (You can see in the preceding code that Pixi's `scale.set` method has been used to make the sprite three times larger than the original image on the tileset, just so it's easier to see.)

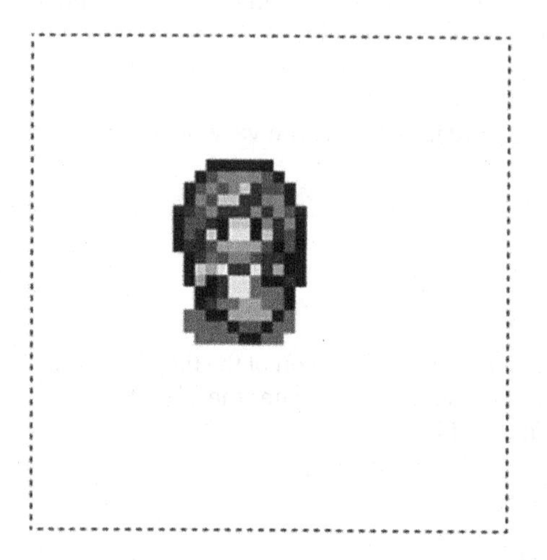

Figure 1-10. *The single image that has been extracted from the tileset*

How does this work? Pixi has a built-in `Rectangle` object (`PIXI.Rectangle`) that is a general-purpose object for defining rectangular shapes. It takes four arguments. The first two arguments define the rectangle's `x` and `y` position. The last two define its `width` and `height`. Here's the general format for defining a new `Rectangle` object:

```
let rectangle = new Rectangle(x, y, width, height);
```

The rectangle object is just a **data object**. That means it's not an image of a rectangle; it's just four numbers that define the position and size of an imaginary rectangle. It's up to you to decide how you want to use that data. In our example, we're using it to define the position and area of the sub-image on the tileset that we want to extract.

Pixi textures have a useful property called `frame` that can be set to any `Rectangle` object. The `frame` crops the texture to the dimensions of the `Rectangle`. Here's how to use `frame` to crop the texture to the size and position of the sub-image you want to extract.

```
let rectangle = new Rectangle(160, 256, 32, 32);
texture.frame = rectangle;
```

You can then use that cropped texture to create the sprite.

```
let adventuress = new Sprite(texture);
```

Figure 1-11 illustrates how this code works.

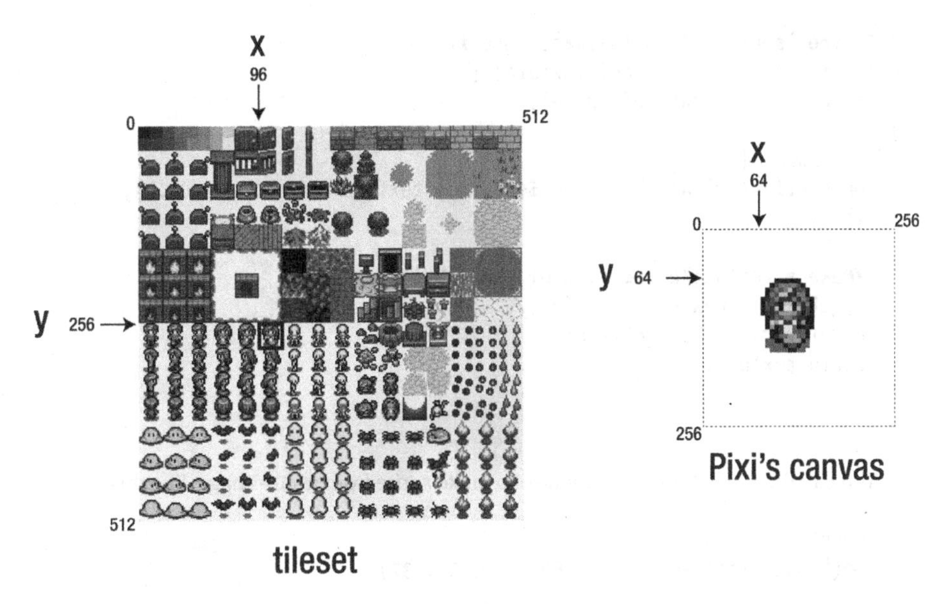

Figure 1-11. Extracting a sub-image from a tileset

■ **Note** Extracting sub-images from a single tileset such as this is a display technique called **blitting** (from the old computer graphics technique: ***b**it b**l**ock **i**mage **t**ransfer*, or "blit," for short).

As creating a sprite such as this from a single tileset image is such a common task, I recommend that you use a convenient custom function called `frame`, to help you automate this. Here's the `frame` function:

```
function frame(source, x, y, width, height) {

  let texture, imageFrame;

  //If the source is a string, it's either a texture in the
  //cache or an image file
  if (typeof source === "string") {
    if (TextureCache[source]) {
      texture = new Texture(TextureCache[source]);
    }
  }
```

```
  //If the `source` is a texture,  use it
  else if (source instanceof Texture) {
    texture = new Texture(source);
  }
  if(!texture) {
    console.log(`Please load the ${source} texture into the cache.`);
  } else {

    //Make a rectangle the size of the sub-image
    imageFrame = new Rectangle(x, y, width, height);
    texture.frame = imageFrame;
    return texture;
  }
}
```

You can then use the `frame` function to make sprite from a sub-image, like this:

```
let adventuress = new Sprite(
  frame("images/tileset.png", 160, 256, 32, 32)
);
```

The first argument is the tileset image. The next four arguments refer to the x, y, width, and height values of the sub-image you want to extract.

■ **Note** You'll find the `frame` function, along with a host of other help functions for working with sprites, in the `library/spriteUtilities` folder in this book's source files.

Preventing Texture Bleed

Unfortunately, GPUs don't always accurately know where one pixel begins and ends. That can produce a graphic glitch called **texture bleed**. Texture bleed is where a portion of a neighboring image is unintentionally extracted in addition to the main image. Figure 1-12 shows a typical example.

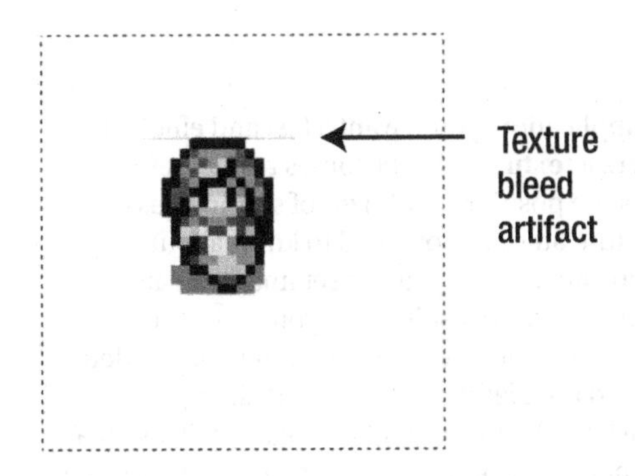

Figure 1-12. *An example of texture bleed*

■ **Note** Texture bleed glitches such as this are often called **artifacts**.

The thin line above the sprite's head is actually part of the image just above it on the tileset.

Take a close look at the tileset we've been using in these examples (Figure 1-11), and you'll see that all the sub-images are jammed together, with no space between them. That means that each sub-image has to be extracted with pixel-perfect precision, so that no fragments of bordering images are accidentally displayed. Unfortunately, GPUs don't have pixel-perfect accuracy. Instead of using perfect integers to refer to pixel positions, GPUs work exclusively with floating-point (decimal) numbers. That means a pixel position might have a precise integer value of 10, but, to the GPU, it might have a less precise floating-point value of 9.989087898909. And, unfortunately, there's no consistency among different GPUs as to how they decide to round up or down.

But there is a solution! You can change the algorithm that the GPU uses to extract pixels. Here's the line of code you need to make sure the GPU rounds to perfect pixel values:

```
texture.baseTexture.scaleMode = PIXI.SCALE_MODES.NEAREST;
```

The texture in this code refers to the tileset that you're extracting your sub-images from. No more texture bleed!

■ **Note** Use `SCALE_MODE.LINEAR`, if you want to set Pixi back to using floating-point values for scaling.

Using a Texture Atlas

If you're working on a big, complex game or application, you'll want a fast and efficient way to create sprites from tilesets. This is where a **texture atlas** becomes really useful. A texture atlas is a JSON data file that contains the positions and sizes of sub-images on a matching tileset PNG image. If you use a texture atlas, all you need to know about the sub-image you want to display is its name. You can arrange your tileset images in any order, and the JSON file will keep track of their sizes and positions for you. This is really convenient, because it means the sizes and positions of tileset images aren't hard-coded into your game program. If you make changes to the tileset, such as adding images, resizing them, or removing them, just republish the JSON file, and your game will use that data to display the correct images. You won't have to make any changes to your game code.

Pixi is compatible with a standard JSON texture atlas format that is output by a popular software tool called Texture Packer (`www.codeandweb.com/texturepacker`). Texture Packer's "Essential" license is free. Let's find out how to use it to make a texture atlas and then load the atlas into Pixi.

Creating the Texture Atlas

■ **Note** You don't have to use Texture Packer. Similar tools, such as Shoebox (`renderhjs.net/shoebox`) or spritesheet.js (`github.com/krzysztof-o/spritesheet.js`), output PNG and JSON files in the same standard format that is compatible with Pixi.

First, start with a collection of individual image files that you'd like to use. Figure 1-13 shows some that you might want to use for a dungeon adventure game.

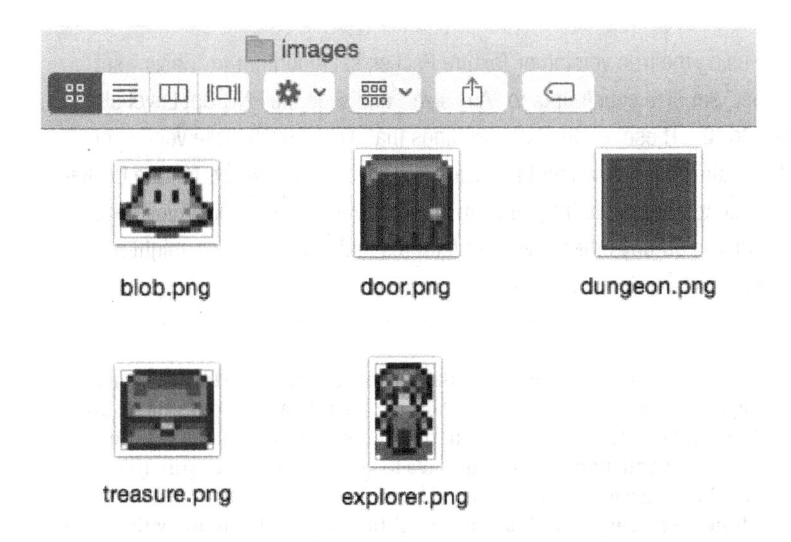

Figure 1-13. *Individual images that you want to add to the texture atlas*

Next, open Texture Packer and choose **JSON Hash** as the framework type. Drag your images into Texture Packer's workspace. (Alternatively, you can point Texture Packer to any folder that contains your images.) It will automatically arrange the images on a single tileset image and give them names that match their original image names. Figure 1-14 shows what you'll see.

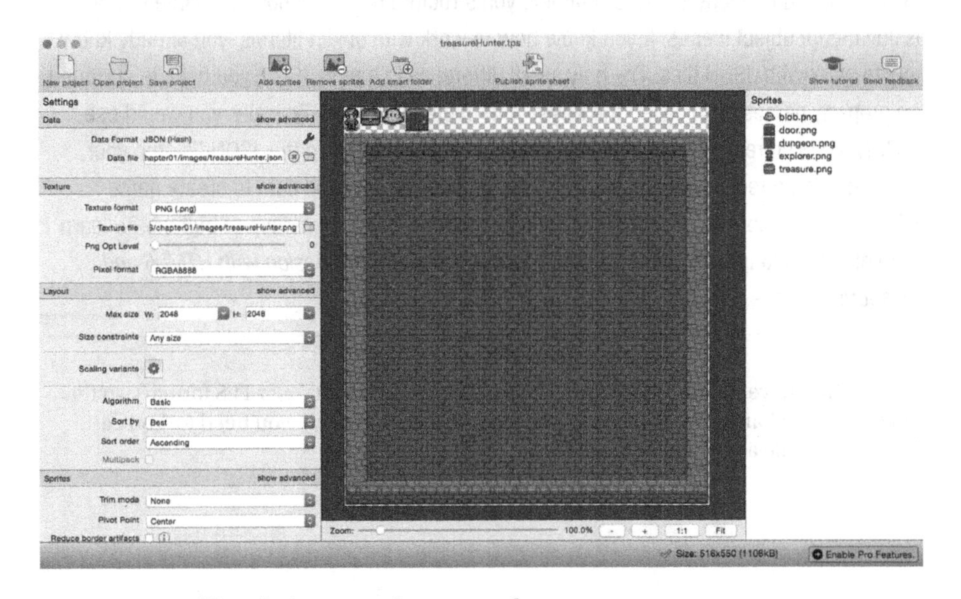

Figure 1-14. *Adding the images to the texture atlas*

■ **Note** If you're using the free version of Texture Packer, set Algorithm to "Basic," set Trim mode to "None," set Size constraints to "Any size," and slide the PNG Opt Level all the way to the left, to "0." These are the basic settings that will allow the free version of Texture Packer to create your files without any warnings or errors. However, Texture Packer changes these precise requirements frequently in new software updates, so, if you have any problems, try turning off any other advanced features that Texture Packer might have switched on in the current version you're using.

In the Data file field, give the texture atlas a name, and give it a save location that's the same as the images you imported to Texture Packer. (That means if your images were in a folder called "images," set the save location to that same "images" folder.) In the Texture file field, enter the same name and same save location. This will ensure that all the texture atlas files share the same name and will be in the same folder.

When you're done, click the "Publish sprite sheet" button. You'll end up with two new files: a PNG file and a JSON data file. In this example, my file names are `treasureHunter.json` and `treasureHunter.png`. If you followed my suggestions in the previous paragraph, they'll be in the same folder. (You can think of the JSON file as extra metadata for the image file, so it makes sense to keep both files in the same folder.)

■ **Note** In case you haven't used them before, JSON (JavaScript Object Notation) files are a very simple data storage format that lets you structure data in almost the same format as JavaScript object literals. If you know how to work with object literals, you already know how to work with JSON files. The only small difference is that in JSON, you have to surround the property names (also called the **keys**) with quotation marks. Typically, you would use a JSON file to store all the data for your game or application, load the JSON file into your program using a technology called XHR, and then use that loaded data to create game objects, such as sprites, or UI (User Interface) elements, such as menus or buttons. To learn more about working with JSON and XHR, see *Advanced Game Design with HTML5 and JavaScript* (Apress, 2015).

You also have to save the Texture Packer file (which is in its own TPS format), so that you can make changes to, and republish, the texture atlas later, if you need to. You can save that TPS file anywhere you like.

The JSON file that Texture Packer produces describes the name, size, and position of each of the sub-images in the tileset. Here's an excerpt that describes the blob monster sub-image:

```
"blob.png":
{
  "frame": {"x":55,"y":2,"w":32,"h":24},
  "rotated": false,
  "trimmed": false,
  "spriteSourceSize": {"x":0,"y":0,"w":32,"h":24},
  "sourceSize": {"w":32,"h":24},
  "pivot": {"x":0.5,"y":0.5}
},
```

The `treasureHunter.json` file also contains `dungeon.png`, `door.png`, `exit.png`, and `explorer.png` properties, each with similar data. Each of these sub-images is called a **frame**. Having this data is really helpful, because now you don't have to know the size and position of each sub-image in the tileset. All you must know is the sprite's **frame id**. The frame id is just the name of the original image file, such as `blob.png` or `explorer.png`.

■ **Note** Among the many advantages to using a texture atlas is that Texture Packer adds two pixels of padding around each image by default. This prevents any danger of texture bleed.

Now that you know how to create a texture atlas, let's find out how to load it into your application code.

Loading the Texture Atlas

Use Pixi's `loader` to import the texture atlas JSON file into your code. If the JSON file was made with Texture Packer, the `loader` will interpret the data and create a texture from each frame on the tileset automatically. Here's how to use the `loader` to load the `treasureHunter.json` file that we created in the previous section. When it has loaded, the `setup` function will run.

```
loader
  .add("images/treasureHunter.json")
  .load(setup);
```

You only have to load the one JSON file. Pixi automatically loads the matching PNG file for you in the background and copies each individual image into the texture cache. You can access each texture in the cache with the same name it had in Texture Packer: `blob.png`, `dungeon.png`, `explorer.png`, and so on.

Creating Sprites from a Loaded Texture Atlas

Pixi gives you two general ways to create a sprite from a texture atlas:

1. Using TextureCache, as follows:

```
let texture = TextureCache["frameId.png"],
    sprite = new Sprite(texture);
```

2. If you've used Pixi's loader to load the texture atlas, use the loader's resources, as follows:

```
let sprite = new Sprite(
  resources["images/treasureHunter.json"].textures["frameId.png"]
);
```

That's way too much typing to have to do just to create a sprite! So, I suggest that you create an alias, called id, that points to texture atlas's textures object, like this:

```
let id = PIXI.loader.resources["images/treasureHunter.json"].textures;
```

Then you can just create each new sprite like this:

```
let sprite = new Sprite(id["frameId.png"]);
```

Much better!

Here's how you could use these different sprite-creation techniques in the setup function that will run after you've loaded the texture atlas. The code creates and displays the dungeon, explorer, door, and treasure sprites.

```
//Define variables that might be used in more than one function
let dungeon, explorer, treasure, door;

function setup() {

  //There are two basic ways to create sprites from loaded texture
  //atlases:
  //1. Access the `TextureCache` directly
  let dungeonTexture = TextureCache["dungeon.png"];
  dungeon = new Sprite(dungeonTexture);
  stage.addChild(dungeon);

  //2. Access the texture using the loader's `resources`:
  explorer = new Sprite(
    resources["images/treasureHunter.json"].textures["explorer.png"]
  );
  explorer.x = 68;
```

```
  //Center the explorer vertically
  explorer.y = stage.height / 2 - explorer.height / 2;
  stage.addChild(explorer);

  //3. Create an optional alias called `id` for all the texture atlas
  //frame id textures.
  let id = PIXI.loader.resources["images/treasureHunter.json"].textures;

  //Make the treasure box using the alias
  treasure = new Sprite(id["treasure.png"]);
  stage.addChild(treasure);

  //Position the treasure next to the right edge of the canvas
  treasure.x = stage.width - treasure.width - 48;
  treasure.y = stage.height / 2 - treasure.height / 2;
  stage.addChild(treasure);

  //Make the exit door
  door = new Sprite(id["door.png"]);
  door.position.set(32, 0);
  stage.addChild(door);

  //Render the stage
  renderer.render(stage);
}
```

Figure 1-15 shows what this code displays.

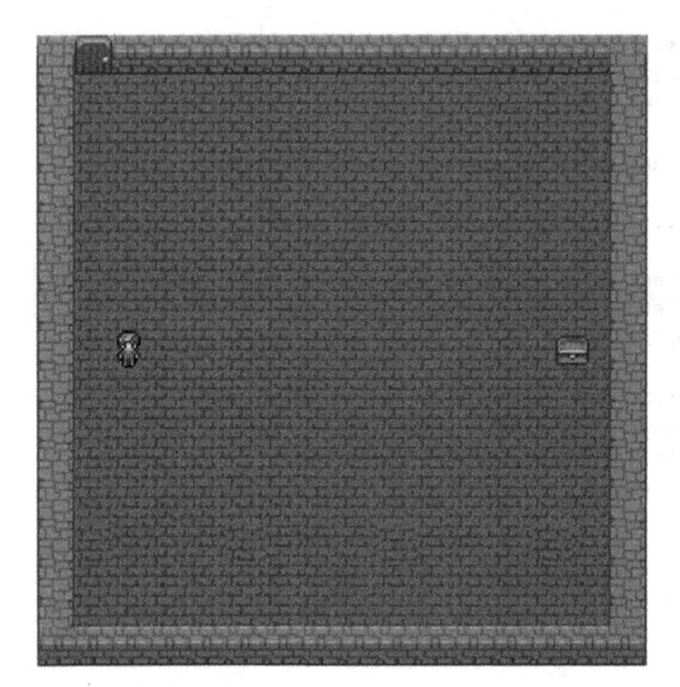

Figure 1-15. Creating sprites using a loaded texture atlas

The stage dimensions are 512 by 512 pixels, and you can see in the preceding code that the `stage.height` and `stage.width` properties are used to align the sprites. Here's how the explorer's y position is centered vertically on the stage:

```
explorer.y = stage.height / 2 - explorer.height / 2;
```

The `treasure` box is also centered vertically and offset from the right side of the stage in a similar way.

```
treasure.x = stage.width - treasure.width - 48;
treasure.y = stage.height / 2 - treasure.height / 2;
```

■ **Note** The `width` and `height` of the root stage container object will be the same as that of the largest sprites that it contains. It is important to note that these values could be different from the width and height of Pixi's renderer. Often, they'll be same, but not necessarily! If you have to know the exact width and height of the renderer, use `renderer.view.width` and `renderer.view.height`.

Making the Blob Monsters

We now want to add six blob monsters to the scene, space them evenly, and give them random y positions. Here's all the code you need to write to do this. Add it to the `setup` function, just before you render the stage.

```
//Make the blobs
let numberOfBlobs = 6,
    spacing = 48,
    xOffset = 150;

//Make as many blobs as there are `numberOfBlobs`
for (let i = 0; i < numberOfBlobs; i++) {

  //Make a blob
  let blob = new Sprite(id["blob.png"]);

  //Space each blob horizontally according to the `spacing` value.
  //`xOffset` determines the point from the left of the screen
  //at which the first blob should be added
  let x = spacing * i + xOffset;

  //Give the blob a random y position
  //(`randomInt` is a custom function - see ahead)
  let y = randomInt(0, stage.height - blob.height);

  //Set the blob's position
  blob.x = x;
  blob.y = y;

  //Add the blob sprite to the stage
  stage.addChild(blob);
}
```

Figure 1-16 shows what this new code produces.

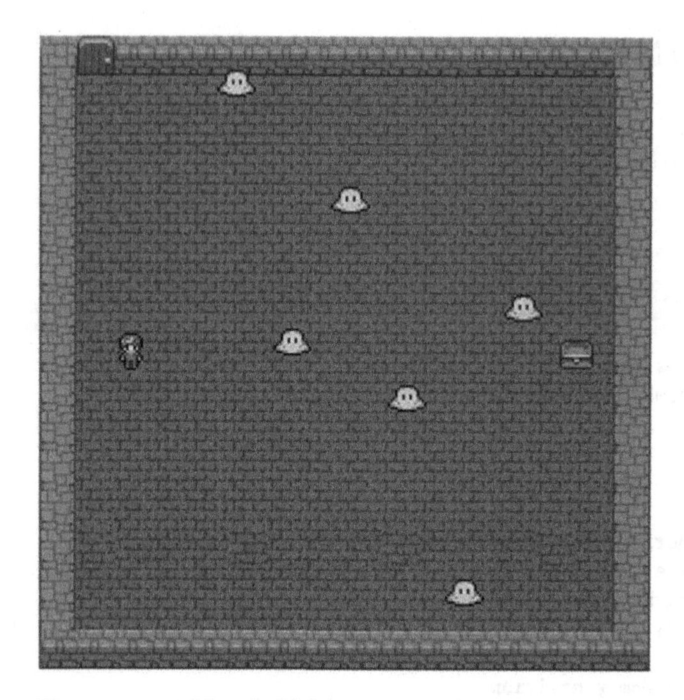

Figure 1-16. *Adding the blob monsters to the scene*

You can see in the preceding code that all the blobs are created by using a good old JavaScript `for` loop. Each `blob` is spaced evenly along the x axis, like this:

```
let x = spacing * i + xOffset;
blob.x = x;
```

`spacing` has a value 48, and `xOffset` has a value of 150. What this means is that the first blob will have an x position of 150. This offsets it from the left side of the stage by 150 pixels. Each subsequent blob will have an x value that's 48 pixels greater than the blob created in the previous iteration of the loop. This creates an evenly spaced line of blob monsters, from left to right, along the dungeon floor.

Each `blob` is also given a random y position, using a custom function called `randomInt`. Here's the code that does this:

```
let y = randomInt(0, stage.height - blob.height);
blob.y = y;
```

The blob's y position could be assigned any random number between 0 and 512, which is the value of `stage.height`. `randomInt` returns a random number that's within a range between any two numbers you supply.

```
randomInt(lowestNumber, highestNumber)
```

This means that if you want a random number between one and ten, you can get one like this:

```
var randomNumber = randomInt(1, 10);
```

Here's the `randomInt` function definition that does all this work:

```
function randomInt(min, max) {
  return Math.floor(Math.random() * (max - min + 1)) + min;
}
```

`randomInt` is a great little helper function to keep in your back pocket for making games. I use it all the time.

The Complete Code

Learning to create and display sprites using a texture atlas is an important benchmark and the way to load and use images with Pixi. So, before I end this chapter, let's take a look at the entire code that creates this dungeon adventure scene. This code uses all the techniques covered in this book so far, so it's a great little summary of everything you've learned.

First, you need a containing HTML document, to host your JavaScript code, and to load Pixi. Here's the HTML code, from the example in the chapter's source code files, that does this:

```
<!doctype html>
<meta charset="utf-8">
<title>Sprite from texture atlas</title>
<body>
<script src="../library/plugins/pixi.js/bin/pixi.js"></script>
<script src="es6spriteFromTextureAtlas.js"></script>
</body>
```

■ **Note** The file paths in the preceding code are the same as the file paths in this book's sample source files. Your own file paths might be different, depending on how you've set up your project folders.

Here's the complete `spriteFromTextureAtlas.js` file that loads the texture atlas and creates the sprites:

```
//Aliases
let Container = PIXI.Container,
    autoDetectRenderer = PIXI.autoDetectRenderer,
    loader = PIXI.loader,
    resources = PIXI.loader.resources,
```

```
    TextureCache = PIXI.utils.TextureCache,
    Texture = PIXI.Texture,
    Sprite = PIXI.Sprite;

//Create a Pixi stage and renderer and add the
//renderer.view to the DOM
let stage = new Container(),
    renderer = autoDetectRenderer(512, 512);
document.body.appendChild(renderer.view);

//Load an image and run the `setup` function when it's done
loader
  .add("images/treasureHunter.json")
  .load(setup);

//Define variables that might be used in more
//than one function
let dungeon, explorer, treasure, door, id;

function setup() {

  //There are two basic ways to create sprites from loaded texture
  //atlases:
  //1. Access the `TextureCache` directly
  let dungeonTexture = TextureCache["dungeon.png"];
  dungeon = new Sprite(dungeonTexture);
  stage.addChild(dungeon);

  //2. Access the texture using throuhg the loader's `resources`:
  explorer = new Sprite(
    resources["images/treasureHunter.json"].textures["explorer.png"]
  );
  explorer.x = 68;

  //Center the explorer vertically
  explorer.y = stage.height / 2 - explorer.height / 2;
  stage.addChild(explorer);

  //Create an optional alias called `id` for all the texture atlas
  //frame id textures.
  let id = PIXI.loader.resources["images/treasureHunter.json"].textures;

  //Make the treasure box using the alias
  treasure = new Sprite(id["treasure.png"]);
  stage.addChild(treasure);
```

```
  //Position the treasure next to the right edge of the canvas
  treasure.x = stage.width - treasure.width - 48;
  treasure.y = stage.height / 2 - treasure.height / 2;
  stage.addChild(treasure);

  //Make the exit door
  door = new Sprite(id["door.png"]);
  door.position.set(32, 0);
  stage.addChild(door);

  //Make the blobs
  let numberOfBlobs = 6,
      spacing = 48,
      xOffset = 150;

  //Make as many blobs as there are `numberOfBlobs`
  for (let i = 0; i < numberOfBlobs; i++) {

    //Make a blob
    let blob = new Sprite(id["blob.png"]);

    //Space each blob horizontally according to the `spacing` value.
    //`xOffset` determines the point from the left of the screen
    //at which the first blob should be added.
    let x = spacing * i + xOffset;

    //Give the blob a random y position
    //(`randomInt` is a custom function - see below)
    let y = randomInt(0, stage.height - blob.height);

    //Set the blob's position
    blob.x = x;
    blob.y = y;

    //Add the blob sprite to the stage
    stage.addChild(blob);
  }

  //Render the stage
  renderer.render(stage);
}

//The `randomInt` helper function
function randomInt(min, max) {
  return Math.floor(Math.random() * (max - min + 1)) + min;
}
```

Summary

Congratulations, you've just completed the most important chapter in the book! The key to working with Pixi is to get comfortable creating a renderer, loading images, turning those image into sprites, and then using sprite properties to position them and change their size. In this chapter, you've learned how to create a Pixi renderer, customize and scale it, and how to set it up for Canvas Drawing API or WebGL rendering. You learned all about Pixi's flexible `loader` object and multiple ways of loading images and turning images into sprites. You've also learned everything you need to know about how to create a texture atlas and use texture atlas frames to create sprites. Now that you know how to do all this, the rest is really just detail.

Pixi is a tool for creating interactive motion graphics, but so far, none of our sprites is moving. That's what the next chapter is all about: making sprites move.

CHAPTER 2

Moving Sprites

You now know how to make sprites, but how do you make them move? That's what this chapter is all about. We're going to take a close look at all the code you have to write to start making your sprites move around the stage. You'll learn about

- Making a game loop
- Using velocity properties
- Modularizing your animation code by using game states
- Making a sprite move by using the keyboard
- Containing a sprite's movement inside the canvas
- Applying physics to a sprite's movement

At the end of this chapter, you'll be well prepared to apply these techniques to all kinds of interactive games and applications, so let's get started!

Create a Game Loop

The first thing you must do to make sprites move is to create a **game loop**. A game loop is just a function that is called, repeatedly, 60 times per second.

Note "Times per second" is more properly referred to as "**frames per second**," or **fps**. Each **frame** is a single unit of movement. You can think of a frame as one page from a hand-drawn animation flip-book. If you flip through the pages (frames!) quickly, your brain is tricked into thinking that many still images are actually one moving image. (This illusion is called **persistence of vision**.)

Any code that you put inside the game loop will also be updated to 60 frames per second. You can make a game loop by using a special JavaScript function called `requestAnimationFrame`. `requestAnimationFrame` tells the browser to update any function you specify at a rate that matches the refresh rate of the computer monitor or device screen that your game or application is running on. The result is that your sprites will move with the smoothest possible animation that your system is capable of producing.

Let's look at some code that shows you how to use `requestAnimationFrame` to make a sprite called `pixie` move from the left side of the canvas to the right side. Figure 2-1 shows what this code produces.

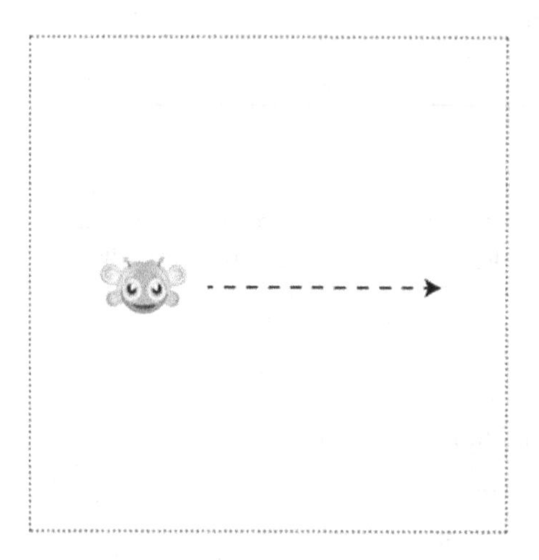

Figure 2-1. *Making a sprite move from left to right*

```
function gameLoop(){

  //Loop this function 60 times per second
  requestAnimationFrame(gameLoop);

  //Move the sprite 1 pixel per frame
  pixie.x += 1;

  //Render the stage
  renderer.render(stage);
}

//Call the `gameLoop` function once to get it started
gameLoop();
```

How does this code work? You can see that the name of this function is `gameLoop`. The `gameLoop` function calls `requestAnimationFrame` and provides itself as an argument.

```
requestAnimationFrame(gameLoop);
```

This is what makes the function run in a continuous loop, at approximately 60 times per second.

To make the sprite move, all you have to do is add a value to the sprite's position. Adding a value of one to the sprite's x position each time the loop is updated will make the sprite move to the right at a rate of one pixel per frame.

```
pixie.x += 1;
```

This is what makes the sprite gradually move from left to right. If you want to make the sprite move faster, use a bigger number, such as 3 or 5. If you want the sprite to move in the opposite direction (from right to left), use a negative number, such as -1 or -4. If you want the sprite to move down, add a positive number to the sprite's y property. If you want it to move up, add a negative number to the sprite's y property.

But, don't forget your last step: *make sure you render the* `stage`:

```
renderer.render(stage);
```

If you don't render the `stage`, you won't see anything!

And that's really all there is to it! Just change any sprite property by small increments inside the loop, and it will animate over time. Here's the complete JavaScript code that loads the image, creates the sprite, and makes it move.

```
//Create a Pixi stage and renderer
let stage = new Container(),
  renderer = autoDetectRenderer(512, 512);
document.body.appendChild(renderer.view);

//Set the canvas's border style and background color
renderer.view.style.border = "1px dashed black";
renderer.backgroundColor = "0xFFFFFF";

//load an image and run the `setup` function when it's done
loader
  .add("images/pixie96x48.png")
  .load(setup);

//Define any variables that are used in more than one function
let pixie;

function setup() {

  //Create the `pixie` sprite
  pixie = new Sprite(resources["images/pixie96x48.png"].texture);

  //Center the sprite vertically on the stage
  pixie.y = renderer.view.height / 2 - pixie.height / 2;

  //Add the sprite to the stage
  stage.addChild(pixie);
```

```
  //Start the game loop
  gameLoop();
}

function gameLoop(){

  //Loop this function 60 times per second
  requestAnimationFrame(gameLoop);

  //Move the sprite 1 pixel per frame
  pixie.x += 1;

  //Render the stage
  renderer.render(stage);
}
```

■ **Note** Notice that the `pixie` sprite variable has to be defined outside the `setup` and `gameLoop` functions, so that you can access it inside both of them.

You can animate a sprite's `scale`, `rotation`, or `width` and `height`—whatever! You'll see many more examples of how to animate sprites ahead.

Using Velocity Properties

To give you more flexibility, it's a good idea to control a sprite's movement speed, using two **velocity properties**: vx and vy. vx is used to set the sprite's speed and direction on the x axis (horizontally). vy is used to set the sprite's speed and direction on the y axis (vertically). Instead of changing a sprite's x and y values directly, first update the velocity variables, and then assign those velocity values to the sprite. This is an extra bit of modularity that you'll need for interactive game animation.

The first step is to create vx and vy properties on your sprite and give them an initial value.

```
pixie.vx = 0;
pixie.vy = 0;
```

Setting vx and vy to 0 means that the sprite isn't moving.

Next, inside the game loop, update vx and vy with the velocity that you want the sprite to move at. Then assign those values to the sprite's x and y properties.

```
pixie.vx = 1;
pixie.vy = 1;

pixie.x += pixie.vx;
pixie.y += pixie.vy;
```

This will make the sprite move down and to the right at one pixel each frame. Here are the new `setup` and `gameLoop` functions that use this new code to produce the effect you can see in Figure 2-2.

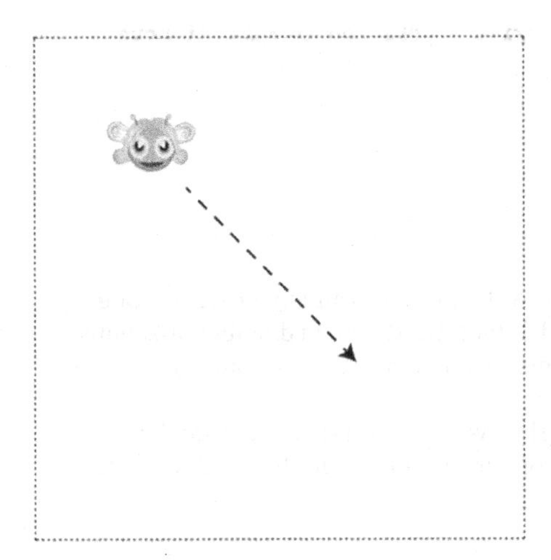

Figure 2-2. *Making a sprite move down and to the right*

```
function setup() {

  //Create the `pixie` sprite
  pixie = new Sprite(resources["images/pixie96x48.png"].texture);

  //Position the sprite at the top left corner
  pixie.x = 0;
  pixie.y = 0;

  //Initialize the sprites's velocity variables
  pixie.vx = 0;
  pixie.vy = 0;

  //Add the sprite to the stage
  stage.addChild(pixie);

  //Start the game loop
  gameLoop();
}

function gameLoop(){

  //Loop this function 60 times per second
  requestAnimationFrame(gameLoop);
```

```
  //Update the sprite's velocity
  pixie.vx = 1;
  pixie.vy = 1;

  //Apply the velocity values to the sprite's position to make it move
  pixie.x += pixie.vx;
  pixie.y += pixie.vy;

  //Render the stage
  renderer.render(stage);
}
```

When you run this code, the pixie sprite will move down and to the right at one pixel per frame. To make the sprite move at different speeds and in different directions, just change the values of the vx and vy variables in the same way you changed the x and y values in the previous example.

You'll see ahead how modularizing a sprite's velocity with vx and vy velocity properties helps with keyboard and mouse pointer control systems for games, as well as making it easier to implement physics.

Game States

As a matter of style, and to help modularize your code, I recommend structuring your game loop like this:

```
//Set the game's current state to `play`:
let state = play;

function gameLoop() {

  //Loop this function at 60 frames per second
  requestAnimationFrame(gameLoop);

  //Update the current game state:
  state();

  //Render the stage to see the animation
  renderer.render(stage);
}

function play() {

  //Move the sprite 1 pixel to the right each frame
  anySprite.x += 1;
}
```

```
```

(The variable anySprite in this sample code could be the name of any sprite in your program.)

You can see that the gameLoop is calling a function called state 60 times per second. What is the state function? It's been assigned to another function called play, with this code:

```
let state = play;
```

That means that state just points to play. And that means all the code in the play function will also run at 60 times per second whenever state is called inside the gameLoop, like this:

```
state();
```

Yes, I know, this is a bit of a head-swirler! But don't let it scare you, and spend a minute or two walking through in your mind how those functions are connected. Figure 2-3 illustrates visually how all this code fits together.

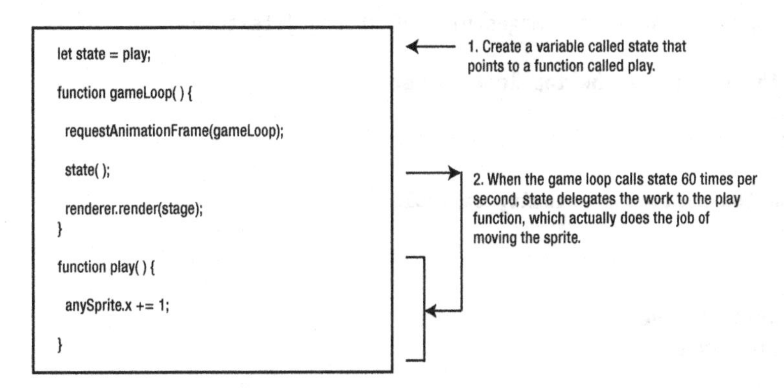

Figure 2-3. *Using states to help modularize your code*

As you'll see ahead, structuring your game loop like this will make it much, much easier to do things such as switching game scenes and levels. It means that you can completely change what your game or application is doing by simply pointing the state variable to any other function that contains the next bit of code you want to run.

```
state = anyOtherFunction;
```

You can do this at any point in your code when you want your application's behavior to change. Because the game loop is just calling the same `state` variable, the behavior will change automatically when you point `state` to a different function. You can use functions from the same JS file, load them with a `<script>` tag, or import them with ES6 modules (or any other module system, such as CommonJS or AMD). In fact, this simple bit of code architecture is the key to scaling your games and applications in a modular and manageable way.

Here's how the code from the previous example can be re-factored to this new model:

```
//Define any variables that are used in more than one function
let pixie;

//Set the game's current state to `play`:
let state = play;

function setup() {

  //Create the `pixie` sprite
  pixie = new Sprite(resources["images/pixie96x48.png"].texture);

  //Position the sprite at the top left corner
  pixie.x = 0;
  pixie.y = 0;

  //Initialize the sprites's velocity variables
  pixie.vx = 0;
  pixie.vy = 0;

  //Add the sprite to the stage
  stage.addChild(pixie);

  //Start the game loop
  gameLoop();
}

function gameLoop(){

  //Loop this function 60 times per second
  requestAnimationFrame(gameLoop);

  //Update the current game state
  state();

  //Render the stage
  renderer.render(stage);
}
```

```
function play() {

  //Update the sprite's velocity
  pixie.vx = 1;
  pixie.vy = 1;

  //Apply the velocity values to the sprite's position to make it move
  pixie.x += pixie.vx;
  pixie.y += pixie.vy;
}
```

Now that we've got a solid model for animating sprites, let's add a few more features: keyboard control, physics, and limiting the area of movement.

■ **Note** This basic game loop will be all you need for most games or applications. But, for a more full-featured game loop, including fine control over the frame rate, consider using a helper library called Smoothie: `github.com/kittykatattack/smoothie`.

Keyboard Movement

With just a little more work, you can build a simple system to control a sprite, using the keyboard. To simplify your code, I suggest that you use this custom function, called `keyboard`, that listens for and captures keyboard events. It's really just a convenient wrapper function for HTML keyup and keydown events, so that you can keep your application code clutter-free and easier to write and read. Here's the complete `keyboard` function. (You'll also find it at its code repository at `github.com/kittykatattack/keyboard`.)

```
function keyboard(keyCode) {
  let key = {};
  key.code = keyCode;
  key.isDown = false;
  key.isUp = true;
  key.press = undefined;
  key.release = undefined;

  //The `downHandler`
  key.downHandler = event => {
    if (event.keyCode === key.code) {
      if (key.isUp && key.press) key.press();
      key.isDown = true;
      key.isUp = false;
    }
    event.preventDefault();
  };
```

```
  //The `upHandler`
  key.upHandler = event => {
    if (event.keyCode === key.code) {
      if (key.isDown && key.release) key.release();
      key.isDown = false;
      key.isUp = true;
    }
    event.preventDefault();
  };

  //Attach event listeners
  window.addEventListener(
    "keydown", key.downHandler.bind(key), false
  );
  window.addEventListener(
    "keyup", key.upHandler.bind(key), false
  );

  //Return the `key` object
  return key;
}
```

The keyboard function is easy to use. Create a new keyboard object, like this:

```
let keyObject = keyboard(asciiKeyCodeNumber);
```

Its one argument is the ASCII key code number of the keyboard key that you want to listen for. A web search will turn up many lists for all the codes on your computer's keyboard, but the following are the four we'll be using in this chapter:

left arrow: 37

up arrow: 38

right arrow: 39

down arrow: 40

Then assign press and release methods to the keyboard object, like this:

```
keyObject.press = () => {
  //key object pressed
};
keyObject.release = () => {
  //key object released
};
```

Keyboard objects also have `isDown` and `isUp` Boolean properties that you can use to check the state of each key. Have a look at the `keyboardMovement.html` file in this chapter's source code folder to see how you can use this keyboard function to control a sprite, using your keyboard's arrow keys. Run it and use the left, up, down, and right arrow keys to move the sprite around the canvas, as shown in Figure 2-4.

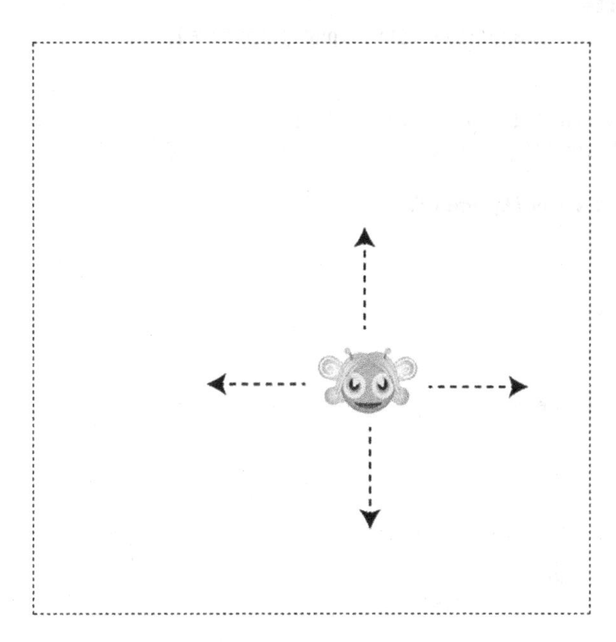

Figure 2-4. *Controlling a sprite with the keyboard*

Here's the complete code that uses the `keyboard` function to create this effect:

```
//Create a Pixi stage and renderer
let stage = new Container(),
  renderer = autoDetectRenderer(512, 512);
document.body.appendChild(renderer.view);

//Set the canvas's border style and background color
renderer.view.style.border = "1px dashed black";
renderer.backgroundColor = "0xFFFFFF";

//load an image and run the `setup` function when it's done
loader
  .add("images/pixie96x48.png")
  .load(setup);
```

```
//Define any variables that are used in more than one function
let pixie, state;

function setup() {

  //Create the `pixie` sprite
  pixie = new Sprite(resources["images/pixie96x48.png"].texture);

  //Center the sprite
  pixie.x = renderer.view.width / 2 - pixie.width / 2;
  pixie.y = renderer.view.height / 2 - pixie.height / 2;

  //Initialize the sprites's velocity variables
  pixie.vx = 0;
  pixie.vy = 0;

  //Add the sprite to the stage
  stage.addChild(pixie);

  //Capture the keyboard arrow keys
  var left = keyboard(37),
      up = keyboard(38),
      right = keyboard(39),
      down = keyboard(40);

  //Left arrow key `press` method
  left.press = () => {

    //Change the sprite's velocity when the key is pressed
    pixie.vx = -5;
    pixie.vy = 0;
  };

  //Left arrow key `release` method
  left.release = () => {

    //If the left arrow has been released, and the right arrow isn't down,
    //and the pixie isn't moving vertically, stop the sprite from moving
    //by setting its velocity to zero
    if (!right.isDown && pixie.vy === 0) {
      pixie.vx = 0;
    }
  };

  //Up
  up.press = () => {
    pixie.vy = -5;
    pixie.vx = 0;
  };
```

```
  up.release = () => {
    if (!down.isDown && pixie.vx === 0) {
      pixie.vy = 0;
    }
  };

  //Right
  right.press = () => {
    pixie.vx = 5;
    pixie.vy = 0;
  };
  right.release = () => {
    if (!left.isDown && pixie.vy === 0) {
      pixie.vx = 0;
    }
  };

  //Down
  down.press = () => {
    pixie.vy = 5;
    pixie.vx = 0;
  };
  down.release = () => {
    if (!up.isDown && pixie.vx === 0) {
      pixie.vy = 0;
    }
  };

  //Set the game's current state to `play`
  state = play;

  //Start the game loop
  gameLoop();
}

function gameLoop(){

  //Loop this function 60 times per second
  requestAnimationFrame(gameLoop);

  //Update the current game state
  state();

  //Render the stage
  renderer.render(stage);
}
```

```
function play() {

  //Apply the velocity values to the sprite's position to make it move
  pixie.x += pixie.vx;
  pixie.y += pixie.vy;
}
```

This code works by first assigning variables to the four keyboard arrow keys:

```
var left = keyboard(37),
    up = keyboard(38),
    right = keyboard(39),
    down = keyboard(40);
```

The `press` and `release` methods for each of those four keys are then programmed. For example, if the user presses the left arrow key, the sprite's horizontal velocity (vx) is set to -5, to make it move left. Its vertical velocity is set to 0, to prevent up or down movement.

```
left.press = () => {
  pixie.vx = -5;
  pixie.vy = 0;
};
```

If the user releases the left arrow key, the sprite's horizontal velocity should be set to 0. But that should only occur if the right arrow key isn't being pressed, and the sprite isn't moving up or down. Here's the code that does all this:

```
left.release = () => {
  if (!right.isDown && pixie.vy === 0) {
    pixie.vx = 0;
  }
};
```

But none of these keys actually makes the sprite move! They just set the correct velocity. The sprite won't move until the `play` function (which runs in the game loop) updates the sprite's x and y position with these velocity values, like this:

```
function play() {
  pixie.x += pixie.vx;
  pixie.y += pixie.vy;
}
```

This is what actually makes the sprite move!

Now that you know the basics of making a sprite move, let's make the effect more interesting, by adding some simple physics.

■ **Note** In Chapter 7, you'll learn how to add mouse and touch interactivity.

Adding Acceleration and Friction

Acceleration is a physics effect that makes a sprite gradually speed up. Friction is an effect that makes the sprite gradually slow down. You can apply acceleration and friction to your keyboard-controlled sprite, so that when you press a key, the sprite gradually speeds up, and when you release a key, it gradually slows down.

The first step is to add acceleration and friction properties to the sprite object. Each axis (x and y) requires its own acceleration and friction property.

```
pixie.accelerationX = 0;
pixie.accelerationY = 0;
pixie.frictionX = 1;
pixie.frictionY = 1;
```

You also need a number that represents the speed at which the sprite should accelerate and a number that represents the amount of drag that will slow the sprite down.

```
pixie.speed = 0.2;
pixie.drag = 0.98;
```

The `speed` value is going to be used to set the acceleration, and the `drag` value is going to be used to set the friction.

The next step is to configure the `press` and `release` methods, so that they set the correct acceleration and friction on the sprite. If the user presses the left key, for example, you want to set `accelerationX` to the negative value of speed (to make the sprite move left). And you want to set friction to 1, which essentially means "don't apply friction while the sprite is accelerating."

```
left.press = () => {
  pixie.accelerationX = -pixie.speed;
  pixie.frictionX = 1;
};
```

■ **Note** Why set friction to 1? As you'll soon see, the `frictionX` and `frictionY` values are **multipliers**. Any value multiplied by 1 means that the value will be unchanged. For example: 1 times 5 equals 5, right? So a friction value of 1 means "no friction."

If the user releases the left key, and the right key isn't currently being pressed, set the acceleration to 0 to stop the sprite from moving and add drag to the friction.

```
left.release = () => {
  if (!right.isDown) {
    pixie.accelerationX = 0;
    pixie.frictionX = pixie.drag;
  }
};
```

You need to apply this same format to the three remaining keys, as follows:

```
//Up
up.press = () => {
  pixie.accelerationY = -pixie.speed;
  pixie.frictionY = 1;
};
up.release = () => {
  if (!down.isDown) {
    pixie.accelerationY = 0;
    pixie.frictionY = pixie.drag;
  }
};

//Right
right.press = () => {
  pixie.accelerationX = pixie.speed;
  pixie.frictionX = 1;
};
right.release = () => {
  if (!left.isDown) {
    pixie.accelerationX = 0;
    pixie.frictionX = pixie.drag;
  }
};

//Down
down.press = () => {
  pixie.accelerationY = pixie.speed;
  pixie.frictionY = 1;
};
down.release = () => {
  if (!up.isDown) {
    pixie.accelerationY = 0;
    pixie.frictionY = pixie.drag;
  }
};
```

As the last step, you have to use acceleration and friction to make the sprite move inside the looping `play` function. Add the acceleration to the velocity, multiply the velocity by the friction, and then, finally, make the sprite move, by adding the velocity to the sprite's position.

```
function play() {

  //Apply acceleration by adding the acceleration to the sprite's velocity
  pixie.vx += pixie.accelerationX;
  pixie.vy += pixie.accelerationY;

  //Apply friction by multiplying sprite's velocity by the friction
  pixie.vx *= pixie.frictionX;
  pixie.vy *= pixie.frictionY;

  //Apply the velocity to the sprite's position to make it move
  pixie.x += pixie.vx;
  pixie.y += pixie.vy;
}
```

Run the `physics.html` file in the chapter's source code files for a fun interactive example of this code in action. Use the arrow keys to fly the pixie sprite all around the stage, as shown in Figure 2-5. She'll accelerate and decelerate smoothly in all directions.

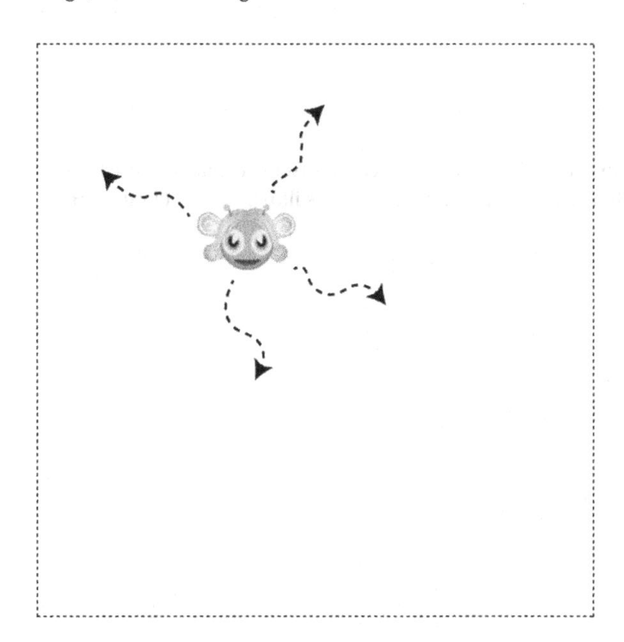

Figure 2-5. *Smooth movement in all directions with acceleration and friction*

The pixie sprite can now fly freely around the canvas, but let's make it a bit more interesting, by adding another important physics property.

Adding Gravity

Gravity is a constant downward force on an object. You can add it to a sprite by applying a constant positive value to the sprite's vertical velocity, like this:

```
pixie.vy += 0.1;
```

You have to add this line of code to the `play` function, along with the other bits of code that help calculate the sprite's velocity. Here's how you could add it to our current example:

```
function play() {

  //Acceleration and friction
  pixie.vx += pixie.accelerationX;
  pixie.vy += pixie.accelerationY;
  pixie.vx *= pixie.frictionX;
  pixie.vy *= pixie.frictionY;

  //Gravity
  pixie.vy += 0.1;

  //Move the sprite
  pixie.x += pixie.vx;
  pixie.y += pixie.vy;
}
```

If you add this code and run the sample file again, you'll discover that you must keep pressing the up key to prevent being pulled down by gravity, as illustrated in Figure 2-6.

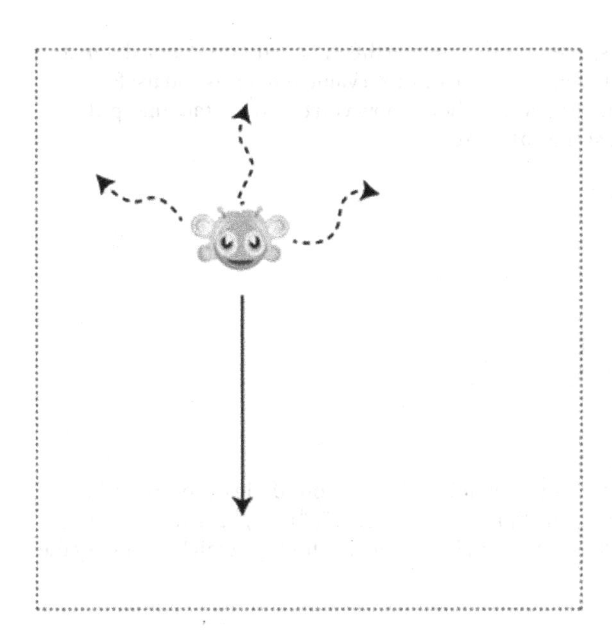

Figure 2-6. *Using gravity to pull the sprite down*

By experimenting with different gravity and `accelerationY` values, you'll be able to fine-tune this effect for an engaging player experience.

■ **Note** This is as much as you need to now to get started using physics with games. For a totally comprehensive exploration of game physics for 2D action games, see this book's companion, *Advanced Game Design with HTML5 and JavaScript* (Apress, 2015).

Containing Movement Inside a Fixed Area

So far, we can make our pixie sprite fly around the canvas, but we have no way of keeping her inside the canvas boundaries. We can fix that by using a special custom function called `contain`. Before you see the code that makes `contain` work, let's find out how to use it. The `contain` function takes two arguments: a sprite and an object literal with `x`, `y`, `width`, and `height` properties. Here's how we could apply it to our `pixie` sprite:

```
contain(pixie, {x: 0, y: 0, width: 512, height: 512});
```

This code will contain the sprite's position inside the 512 by 512 pixel area defined by the object literal. The `contain` function also returns a value that gives you useful information about the collision. For example, here's how you could contain the sprite inside the canvas area and access the `collision` value:

```
let collision = contain(
  pixie,
  {
    x: 0,
    y: 0,
    width: renderer.view.width,
    height: renderer.view.height
  }
);
```

If the sprite bumps into any of the containing object's boundaries, the `collision` value will tell you which side the sprite bumped into: `"left"`, `"top"`, `"right"`, or `"bottom"`. Here's how you could use that `collision` value to find out which boundary the sprite hit.

```
if(collision) {
  if collision.has("left") console.log("The sprite hit the left");
  if collision.has("top") console.log("The sprite hit the top");
  if collision.has("right") console.log("The sprite hit the right");
  if collision.has("bottom") console.log("The sprite hit the bottom");
}
```

If the sprite doesn't hit a boundary, the value of `collision` will be `undefined`.

To see the `contain` function in action, run the `containingMovement.html` example file in this chapter's source code. Use the arrow keys to fly the pixie sprite around, and watch her bounce against the sides of the canvas when she hits them. Figure 2-7 illustrates what you'll see.

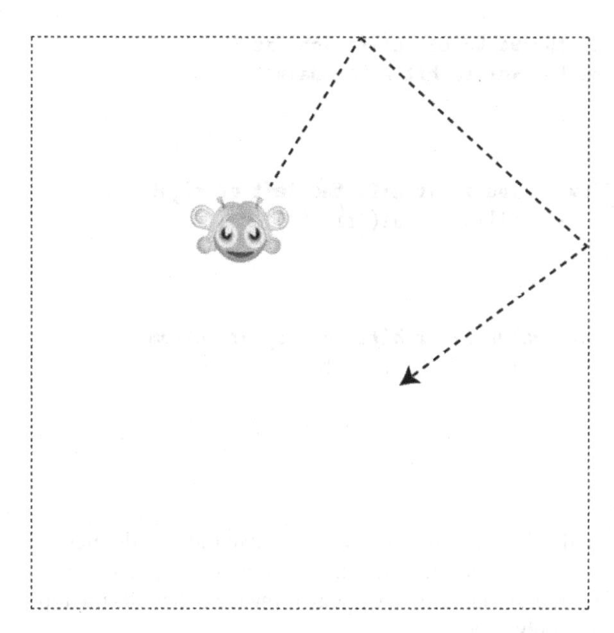

Figure 2-7. *Bouncing the sprite against the sides of the canvas*

Here's the new code from the `play` function that uses `contain` to achieve this effect:

```
function play() {

  //Apply physics to the sprite's position
  pixie.vx += pixie.accelerationX;
  pixie.vy += pixie.accelerationY;
  pixie.vx *= pixie.frictionX;
  pixie.vy *= pixie.frictionY;
  pixie.x += pixie.vx;
  pixie.y += pixie.vy;

  //Use the `contain` function to keep the sprite inside the canvas

  let collision = contain(
    pixie,                              //The sprite you want to contain
    {                                   //An object that defines the area
      x: 0,                             //`x` position
      y: 0,                             //`y` position
      width: renderer.view.width,       //`width`
      height: renderer.view.height      //`height`
    }
  );
```

```
  //Check for a collision. If the value of `collision` isn't
  //`undefined` then you know the sprite hit a boundary

  if (collision) {

    //Reverse the sprite's `vx` value if it hits the left or right
    if (collision.has("left") || collision.has("right")){
      pixie.vx = -pixie.vx;
    }

    //Reverse the sprite's `vy` value if it hits the top or bottom
    if (collision.has("top") || collision.has("bottom")){
      pixie.vy = -pixie.vy;
    }
  }
}
```

The `contain` function automatically keeps the sprite contained in the area defined by the object literal. The bounce effect is achieved by the last two lines of the preceding code. If the sprite hits the left or right boundary, its vx velocity is reversed. If it hits the top or bottom boundary, its vy velocity is reversed.

```
pixie.vx = -pixie.vx;
pixie.vy = -pixie.vy;
```

That's what makes the sprite bounce.

But where do those values, `"left"`, `"top"`, `"right"`, and `"bottom"` come from, and what does `collision.has` mean? Let's find out by taking a quick look at JavaScript sets, and then how they're used in the custom `contain` function.

Using ES6 Sets

The `collision` value that was returned by the `contain` function in the previous example is actually a JavaScript ES6 Set object. A set is similar to an array, but with a few interesting little tweaks. Before we take a look at how the `contain` function works, let's find out what an ES6 `Set` object is and how to use it. Following is a quick-start guide to using ES6 sets.

You can create a set like this:

```
let things = new Set();
```

Set objects are like arrays, and you can populate them with data, like this:

```
let things = new Set(["left", "top", "right", "bottom"]);
```

One of the biggest differences between sets and arrays is that sets can only contain one instance of any value. This is a really good thing and why sets can be really handy for situations in which you don't need or want duplicate values. For example, in an array, you could have the value "left" two or three times. But in a set, you can only have one "left". If you try to add a second or third "left", nothing happens.

You can add a new item to a set with the add method, as follows:

```
things.add("anotherThing");
```

You can remove an item with the delete method.

```
things.delete("right");
```

You can completely empty a set of all its items by using the clear method.

```
things.clear();
```

If you want to find out whether a set contains a value, use the has method.

```
if (things.has("left")) {/* Then do this... */}
```

Using has is a much faster operation than checking whether items exist in an array using indexOf. Sets are optimized for these kinds of look-ups; it's their super-power!

You can also initialize a set with any pre-existing array.

```
let things = new Set(anyArray);
```

That will give you a set that uses the values in the preexisting array, but if there are any duplicate values in the array, they'll be removed from the set. Remember: Sets can only contain unique values.

If you want to find out how many elements are in a set, use the size property.

```
things.size;
```

And if you want to loop through all the elements in an set, use the forEach method.

```
things.forEach(element => console.log(element));
```

This will loop through and display all the elements in a set.

■ **Note** ES6 also has a highly memory-efficient version of sets called `WeakSet`. `WeakSets` let the garbage collector immediately re-use the memory space of any elements in the set that were deleted, even if those elements reference other objects being used somewhere else in your code. This is a great feature, because it can prevent possible memory leaks. The trade-off is that `WeakSet` only supports the `add`, `has`, and `delete` methods. If that's not a problem, it is preferable to use `WeakSet` instead of `Set` anywhere in your code.

Why should you use sets instead arrays or object literals? If you only want or need no more than one kind of value in the set, or want to prevent duplicate values from being added, use a set. If you want a high-performance look-up of values using the `has` method, use a set. If you want to be certain of preventing memory leaks, use a `WeakSet`. If you want more features and more flexibility, use arrays or object literals. Arrays and object literals are cool. We love them, and they're not going anywhere!

OK, got it? Now that you know all about ES6 sets, let's find out how a set was used to create the custom `contain` function we used in the previous example.

The contain Function

The `contain` function has two parameters: the sprite and the container object that defines the `x`, `y`, `width`, and `height` values of the containment areas. The code checks to see if the sprite's x and y position has crossed any of those boundaries. If it has, the sprite is moved back to those boundary limits. A set called `collision` is used to track which boundary side the collision occurred on: `"left"`, `"top"`, `"right"`, or `"bottom"`. The `collision` set is returned by the function. If the sprite didn't touch any of the boundaries, `collision` is set to undefined, to indicate that there was no collision. Here's the complete `contain` function that does all this:

```
function contain(sprite, container) {

  //Create a `Set` called `collision` to keep track of the
  //boundaries with which the sprite is colliding
  var collision = new Set();

  //Left
  //If the sprite's x position is less than the container's x position,
  //move it back inside the container and add "left" to the collision Set
  if (sprite.x < container.x) {
    sprite.x = container.x;
    collision.add("left");
  }
```

```
  //Top
  if (sprite.y < container.y) {
    sprite.y = container.y;
    collision.add("top");
  }

  //Right
  if (sprite.x + sprite.width > container.width) {
    sprite.x = container.width - sprite.width;
    collision.add("right");
  }

  //Bottom
  if (sprite.y + sprite.height > container.height) {
    sprite.y = container.height - sprite.height;
    collision.add("bottom");
  }

  //If there were no collisions, set `collision` to `undefined`
  if (collision.size === 0) collision = undefined;

  //Return the `collision` value
  return collision;
}
```

Keeping sprites contained inside a boundary is a very common task in games and interactive applications, and you'll see many more examples of how the `contain` function is used later in this book. (You'll find the `contain` function in this chapter's source code or its code repository: `github.com/kittykatattack/contain`.)

Summary

You've now got all the basic skills you need to make sprites move. You've learned how to update a sprite's position inside a game loop, how to use velocity variables, and how to apply useful physics properties such as acceleration, friction, and gravity. You also learned how to structure a modular application, by using a state variable to control the program flow. You'll see how useful this will be a little later in this book when our applications become a bit more sophisticated. I've also covered the basics of interactive animation, by using a keyboard controller to move a sprite, and that will prepare you for Chapter 8, which takes a closer look at interactive animation using mouse and touch events. But we're not done with animation yet—far from it! In Chapter 5, you'll learn all about keyframe animation, and in Chapter 6, you'll learn how to create transitions and use tweening effects.

So far in this book, we've looked at how to make sprites using images, but Pixi lets you make sprites just as easily using lines and shapes. Let's find out how, in the next chapter!

CHAPTER 3

Shapes, Text, and Groups

So far in this book, all the sprites we've used have been based on existing images that we loaded into our programs. But Pixi also has its own low-level drawing tools that you can use to make shapes, lines, and text. To help keep things organized, you can group all your shapes and images together, so that you can work with them as a single unit. In this chapter, you're going to learn how to do all that, including:

- Making rectangles, circles, lines, ellipses, and polygons
- Creating text
- Grouping sprites

All the sample code in this chapter is meant to be run inside the `setup` function of the basic Pixi application template you learned to use in Chapter 2. Here's the template; code comments show where to add the code we'll be writing in this chapter:

```
//Create a Pixi stage and renderer
let stage = new Container(),
  renderer = autoDetectRenderer(512, 512);
document.body.appendChild(renderer.view);

//Set the canvas's border style and background color
renderer.view.style.border = "1px dashed black";
renderer.backgroundColor = "0xFFFFFF";

//load resources (images and fonts) and then run the `setup` function
loader
  .add("fonts/puzzler.ttf")
  .load(setup);

//Define any variables that are used in more than one function

//Set the initial game state
let state = play;
```

```
function setup() {

  /*
  All the code for this chapter goes here
  */

  //Start the game loop
  gameLoop();
}

function gameLoop(){

  //Loop this function 60 times per second
  requestAnimationFrame(gameLoop);

  //Run the current state
  state();

  //Render the stage
  renderer.render(stage);
}

function play() {

  //Any animation or game logic code goes here
}
```

Making Shapes

Pixi's application program interface (API) for making shapes and lines is very similar to the HTML Canvas drawing API, so, if you already know how to draw shapes with Canvas, you'll find it very familiar.

■ **Note** For a comprehensive introduction to the Canvas drawing API, see my book *Advanced Game Design with HTML5 and JavaScript* (Apress, 2015).

But Pixi's big advantage is that, unlike the Canvas drawing API, the shapes you draw with Pixi are rendered by WebGL on the graphics processor unit (GPU). Pixi lets you access all that untapped performance power and bundles it into a user-friendly package.

All shapes are made using the same basic format. Following is the basic code you have to write to make most kinds of shapes:

```
//Create a Graphics object
let shape = new Graphics();

//Set the fill color
shape.beginFill(hexColorCode);

//Set the line style
anyShape.lineStyle(lineThickness, hexColorCode, alpha);

//Draw the shape
//Use `drawRect`, `drawCircle`, `drawEllipse`,
//`drawRoundedRect` or `drawPolygon` to draw the shape

//End the color fill
shape.endFill();

//Position the shape
shape.position.set(64, 64);

//Add the shape to the stage
stage.addChild(shape);
```

All the shapes (and lines) are created by first making an instance of Pixi's `Graphics` class (`PIXI.Graphics`).

```
let shape = new Graphics();
```

Then use the `beginFill` method to set fill color for the shape. Use any hexadecimal color code.

```
shape.beginFill(hexColorCode);
```

If you want an outline around your shape, use the `lineStyle` method to set the outline thickness, color, and transparency. (Transparency is usually referred to by the graphics design term **alpha**.)

```
anyShape.lineStyle(lineThickness, hexColorCode, alpha);
```

`lineThickness` is a number, in pixels, that determines how thick you want the line to be. `alpha` is a value between 0 and 1. 0 means the line will be completely transparent; 1 means it will be completely opaque (solid).

Next, use one of Pixi's drawing methods (which you'll learn about ahead!) to draw the shape you want: `drawRect`, `drawCircle`, `drawEllipse`, `drawRoundedRect`, or `drawPolygon`.

Finally, use the `endFill` method to fill the shape with the color.

```
shape.endFill();
```

You can then position the shape on the canvas, using x and y properties, and apply other optional sprite properties such as `alpha` and `scale`.

```
shape.position.set(64, 64);
stage.addChild(shape);
```

■ **Remember** Just as with a normal sprite, you won't be able to see the shape until you add it to the stage.

Let's find out how to use this general format to make basic shapes.

Rectangles

Use the `drawRect` method to draw a rectangle. Its four arguments are x, y, `height`, and `width`.

```
rectangle.drawRect(x, y, width, height);
```

Here's how to draw a blue (0x0033CC) rectangle with a red (0xFF0000) outline, position it, and make it semitransparent:

```
let rectangle = new Graphics();
rectangle.beginFill(0x0033CC);
rectangle.lineStyle(4, 0xFF0000, 1);
rectangle.drawRect(0, 0, 96, 96);
rectangle.endFill();
rectangle.x = 64;
rectangle.y = 64;
rectangle.alpha = 0.5;
stage.addChild(rectangle);
```

Figure 3-1 shows the result of this code.

Figure 3-1. *Drawing a rectangle*

You'll notice that the x and y arguments of the drawRect method are both set to 0.

```
rectangle.drawRect(0, 0, 96, 96);
```

These are the rectangle's **local** x and y positions inside the graphics object. What you really want to do is position the rectangle relative to the canvas's top-left corner: its **global** position. That's why, after the rectangle is drawn, its x and y positions are set to 64 and 64, as follows:

```
rectangle.x = 64;
rectangle.y = 64;
```

I recommend that you adhere to this model, as it gives you a little more flexibility to position your shape in more complex drawing situations.

■ **Note** What's the difference between local and global coordinates? Don't worry too much about that now. It's all explained a little further ahead!

In the preceding code, you can also see that the rectangle is made semitransparent by setting its alpha value to 0.5, as follows:

```
rectangle.alpha = 0.5;
```

If there are any other sprites or shapes under this rectangle, they'll be partially visible.

Rounded Rectangles

If you want a rectangle with rounded corners, use the drawRoundedRect method.

```
rectangle.drawRoundedRect(x, y, width, height, cornerRadius);
```

The last argument, cornerRadius, determines how rounded the corners should be. Here's how to make a rounded rectangle with a corner radius of 12, shown in Figure 3-2:

```
rectangle.drawRoundedRect(0, 0, 96, 96, 12);
```

Figure 3-2. *A rectangle with rounded corners*

Circles

Use the drawCircle method to draw a circle. The first two arguments are the circle's x and y positions, and the third is its radius (the distance from the circle's center to its edge).

```
circle.drawCircle(x, y, radius);
```

Unlike rectangles, a circle's x and y positions refer to its center point. Here's some code that draws an orange (0xFF9933) circle with a radius of 48 pixels and a dark green (0x006600) outline:

```
let circle = new Graphics();
circle.beginFill(0xFF9933);
circle.lineStyle(4, 0x006600, 1);
circle.drawCircle(0, 0, 48);
circle.endFill();
circle.x = 256;
circle.y = 112;
stage.addChild(circle);
```

Figure 3-3 shows what this code produces.

Figure 3-3. *Drawing a circle*

■ **Note** Does the line around the circle in Figure 3-3 look jagged and pixelated to you? It is! You'll learn how to solve this problem in the section ahead on antialiasing.

Ellipses

Pixi also lets you draw an ellipse with the `drawEllipse` method.

```
drawEllipse(x, y, width, height);
```

As with circles, the x/y position defines the ellipse's center point. Here's a yellow (0xFFFF00) ellipse with a black (0x000000) outline that's 64 pixels wide and 32 pixels high, shown in Figure 3-4.

```
let ellipse = new Graphics();
ellipse.beginFill(0xFFFF00);
ellipse.lineStyle(4, 0x000000, 1);
ellipse.drawEllipse(0, 0, 64, 32);
ellipse.endFill();
ellipse.x = 416;
ellipse.y = 112;
stage.addChild(ellipse);
```

Figure 3-4. *Drawing an ellipse*

Straight Lines

If you want to make a straight line, use the lineStyle method to set the line's width, color, and alpha transparency. Then use two new methods, moveTo and lineTo to draw the line. moveTo sets the line's start x/y position, and lineTo is the x/y position of the end point. Following is the code for a 4-pixel-wide black diagonal line. Figure 3-5 shows the result of this code.

```
let line = new Graphics();
line.lineStyle(4, 0x000000, 1);
line.moveTo(0, 0);
line.lineTo(100, 50);
line.x = 64;
line.y = 212;
stage.addChild(line);
```

Figure 3-5. *A diagonal line*

Polygons

You can join lines together and fill them with colors to make complex shapes. Here's how to connect three lines to make a red (0xFF3300) triangle with a blue (0x336699) border. The shape is drawn at position 0,0 and then positioned on the stage using x and y values.

```
let triangle = new Graphics();
triangle.beginFill(0xFF3300);
triangle.lineStyle(4, 0x336699, 1);
triangle.moveTo(0,0);
triangle.lineTo(-64, 64);
triangle.lineTo(64, 64);
triangle.lineTo(0, 0);
triangle.endFill();

//The x/y position refers to the first point of the triangle
triangle.x = 320;
triangle.y = 192;
stage.addChild(triangle);
```

Figure 3-6 illustrates how the moveTo and lineTo methods are used to define the corners of the triangle.

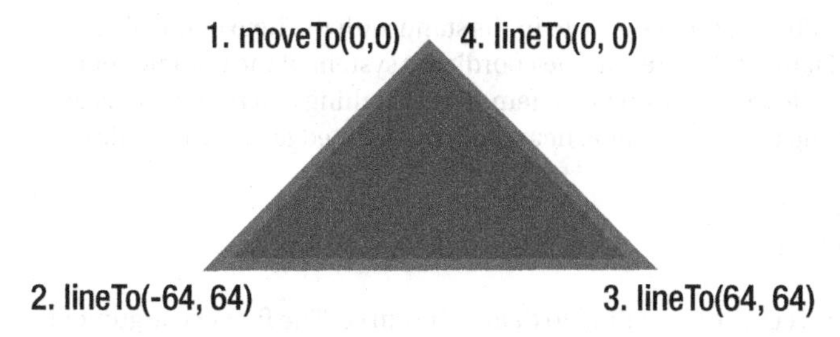

Figure 3-6. *Using `moveTo` and `lineTo` to join lines to form shapes*

Curved Lines

Pixi lets you draw two types of curved lines: **quadratic curves** and **Bezier curves**. It also lets you draw arcs (partial circles) between any two points. Let's find out how.

Quadratic Curves

To draw a quadratic curve, use the `quadraticCurveTo` method. The following code produces the curve you can see in Figure 3-7:

```
let quadLine = new Graphics();
quadLine.lineStyle(4, 0x000000, 1);
quadLine.moveTo(32, 128);
quadLine.quadraticCurveTo(128, 20, 224, 128);
stage.addChild(quadLine);
```

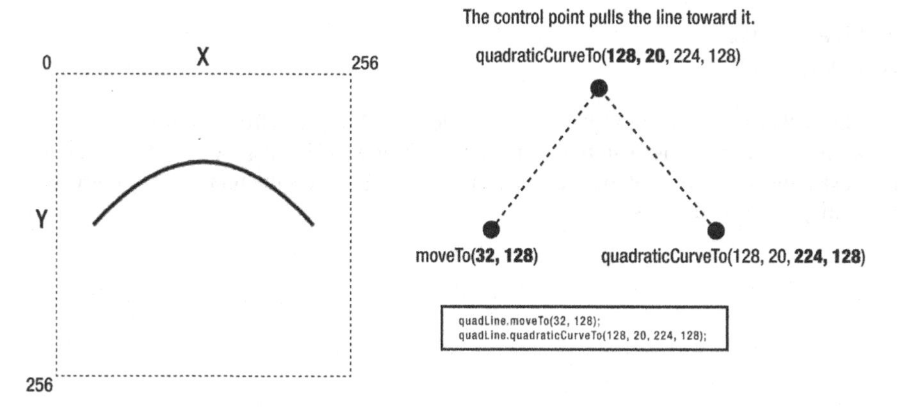

Figure 3-7. *A quadratic curve*

The code alone is confusing, but it's easy to understand with the help of the diagram. The x and y positions in Figure 3-7 represent the coordinate system of the graphics object. We're drawing the line inside that coordinate system. The first thing you have to do is use moveTo to define the starting point of the line, near the left-center edge of the graphics object, as follows:

```
quadLine.moveTo(32, 128);
```

Then use the quadraticCurveTo method to define the curve. The first two arguments define what's known as the **control point**. You can think of the control point as a kind of invisible gravity point that pulls the line toward it. In this example, the control point is near the center top of the graphics object, at an x position of 128 and a y position of 20, which I've highlighted here:

```
quadLine.quadraticCurveTo(128, 20, 224, 128);
```

The last two arguments are the line's end point.

```
quadLine.quadraticCurveTo(128, 20, 224, 128);
```

Can you see in Figure 3-7 how these points work together to create the curve?

Local and Global Coordinates

We've drawn the line inside the Graphics object, and these x and y coordinates are the Graphics object's own internal **local coordinates**. However, we still need to position this Graphics object on Pixi's canvas. The position of the Graphics object is the line's **global coordinates**. Here's how to set them:

```
quadLine.x = 128;
quadLine.y = 128;
```

This will position the line 128 pixels to the left and 128 pixels from the top of Pixi's canvas. If you don't set these global coordinates, the line will be displayed at position 0,0, at the exact top-left corner of Pixi's canvas. Figure 3-8 illustrates the relationship between local and global coordinates.

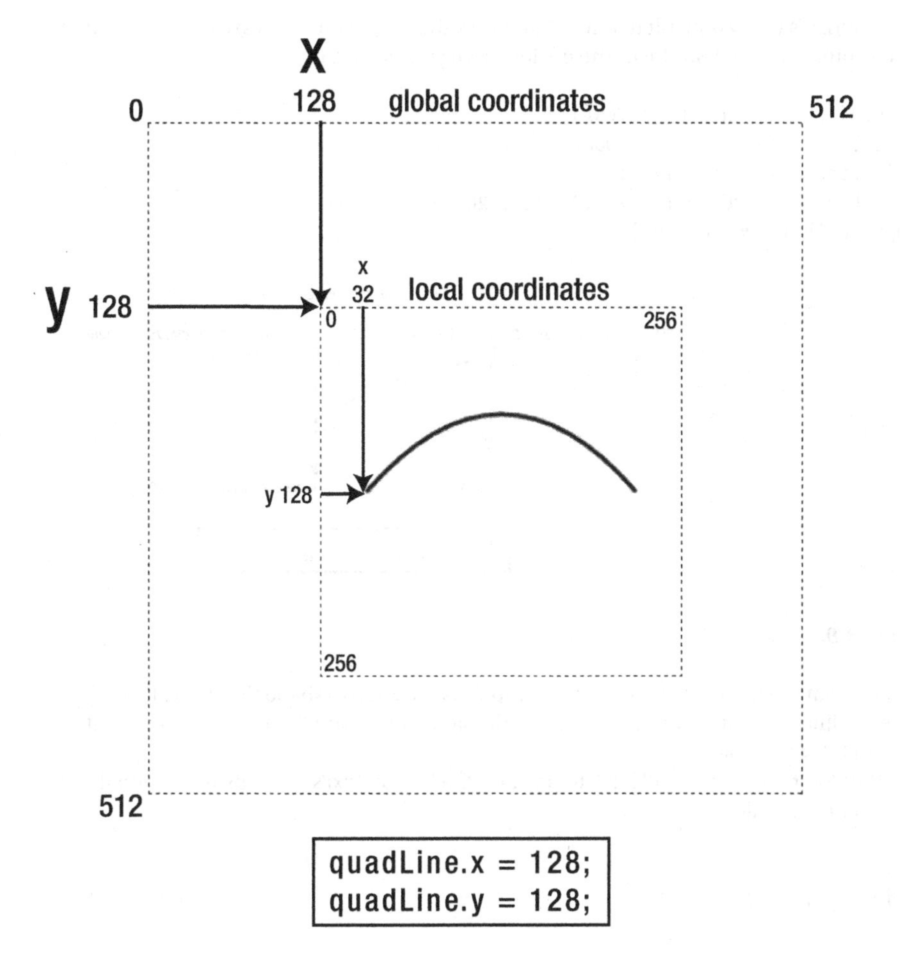

Figure 3-8. *Drawing a line by using local coordinates and positioning it on Pixi's stage by using global coordinates*

Bezier Curves

Bezier curves are similar to quadratic curves, but they add a second control point:

```
bezierCurveTo(control1X, control1Y, control2X, control2Y, endX, endY);
```

Again, it's really difficult to understand how this works until you see a clear example. Here's some code that produces the Bezier curve you can see in Figure 3-9.

```
let bezierLine = new Graphics();
bezierLine.lineStyle(4, 0x000000, 1);
bezierLine.moveTo(32, 128);
bezierLine.bezierCurveTo(32, 20, 224, 20, 224, 128);
stage.addChild(bezierLine);
```

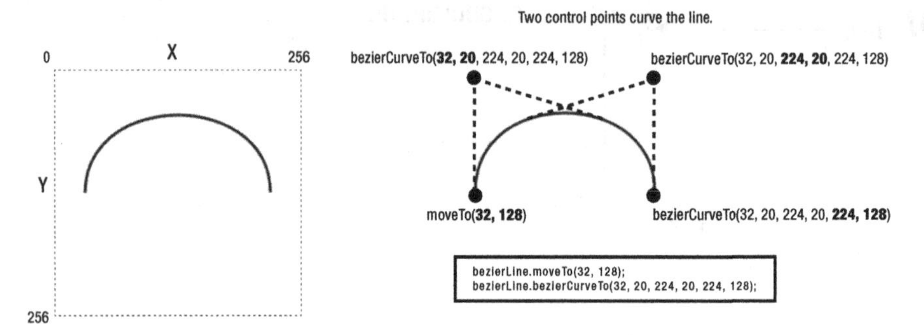

Figure 3-9. *A Bezier curve*

You can see in Figure 3-9 how the four points are used to shape the curve. If you close the lines so that they start and end at the same point, you'll produce a shape that you can fill with a color.

But don't forget! You still have to position the line on Pixi's stage, using its global coordinates, as follows:

```
bezierLine.x = 256;
bezierLine.y = 256;
```

Drawing Arcs

Earlier in this chapter, you learned how to make a circle, using the `drawCircle` method. But if you have to draw a partial circle, you can do this using the `arc` and `arcTo` methods.

The `arc` method lets you draw an arc (a partial circle), using this format:

```
arc(centerX, centerY, circleRadius, startAngle, endAngle, false)
```

The `centerX` and `centerY` coordinates are the circle's center point. The `circleRadius` is a number, in pixels, that determines the circle's radius (half its width). The `startAngle` and `endAngle` are numbers in radians that determine how complete the circle is. For a full circle, use a `startAngle` of 0 and an `endAngle` of 6.28 (`2 * Math.PI`). (The `startAngle`'s 0 position is at the circle's 3 o'clock position.) The last argument, `false`, indicates that the circle should be drawn clockwise from the `startAngle`.

Just use a startAngle greater than 0 and an endAngle less than 6.28 (2 * Math.PI). Here's some code that draws an arc from 3.14 to 5 radians, as shown in Figure 3-10:

```
let partialCircle = new Graphics();
partialCircle.lineStyle(4, 0x000000, 1);
partialCircle.arc(64, 64, 64, 3.14, 5, false);
partialCircle.x = 64;
partialCircle.y = 416;
stage.addChild(partialCircle);
```

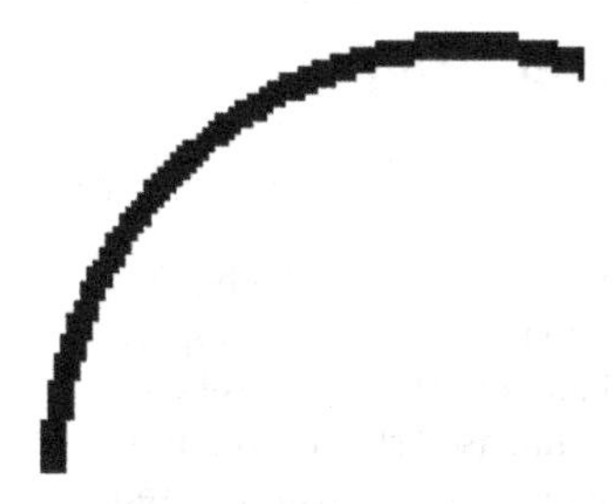

Figure 3-10. *Drawing an arc*

Pixi has an alternative method for drawing arcs called arcTo. Supply arcTo with the arc's start and end points, and then the radius (in pixels) of the arc that you want to draw between those points.

```
arcTo(startX, startY, endX, endY, radius);
```

Use whichever method for drawing arcs that you prefer.

That's it for Pixi's lines and shapes! But before we move on, let's refine some of our techniques for drawing them.

Improving Graphics Rendering

Now that you know how to draw lines and shapes, let's look at some of the tools Pixi offers you to make them look and perform better: WebGL antialiasing, drawing on a single graphics context, and how to clear and redraw graphics.

Antialiasing for WebGL Graphics

If you're using Pixi's WebGL renderer (which is what autoDetectRenderer defaults to), you'll notice that your lines and shapes aren't **antialiased**. What does that mean? Without antialiasing, curved lines and shapes look jagged and pixelated. Antialiasing is a computer graphics algorithm that creates the illusion of smooth curves by adding extra shaded pixels of varying gradations around the shape. It blurs the jaggies. Figure 3-11 illustrates a comparative example of a non-antialiased and antialiased curve.

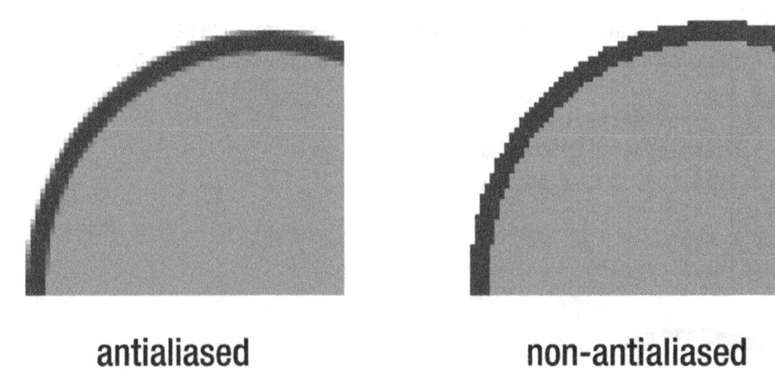

Figure 3-11. Antialiasing produces smooth curves

Pixi's `WebGLRenderer` doesn't antialias lines and shapes. Why? Because WebGL's internal **stencil buffer** (the means Pixi uses to draw lines and shapes) doesn't support antialiasing. This is just a limitation of the WebGL 1.0 specification. However, WebGL's bitmap renderer *does* support antialiasing. So, if you want antialiased shapes, you must first convert your graphics into a bitmap texture and then display that new, antialiased, bitmap texture. Pixi doesn't do this for you automatically, because it's a computationally expensive thing to do, and Pixi wisely optimizes for performance. But, if you need antialiased WebGL graphics, Pixi gives you the tools to make them.

■ **Note** Pixi's `CanvasRenderer` automatically produces antialiased lines and shapes. However, `CanvasRenderer` is usually much slower at drawing graphics than `WebGLRenderer`. (But not always! Test it with your particular setup and see.)

The trick to creating antialiased lines is first to use a Pixi `Graphics` object method called `generateTexture` to create a bitmap texture of the line or shape.

```
let texture = shape.generateTexture();
```

Then, use this new texture to create a sprite.

```
let shapeSprite = new Sprite(texture);
```

Let's look at some code you could write to convert a jaggedy, non-antialiased circle into a smooth, antialiased circle. First, write some familiar code to draw the circle, using Pixi's `Graphics` object.

```
let circle = new Graphics();
circle.beginFill(0xFF9933);
circle.lineStyle(4, 0x006600, 1);
circle.drawCircle(0, 0, 48);
circle.endFill();
```

This is the same code you saw before. Next, use generateTexture to create a texture from the circle, and use that texture to create a sprite.

```
let circleTexture = circle.generateTexture();
let circleSprite = new Sprite(circleTexture);
circleSprite.x = 212;
circleSprite.y = 64;
stage.addChild(circleSprite);
```

You've now got an ordinary Sprite object, called circleSprite, that you can use just like any other sprite you created in the previous chapter. And remember: Sprites have their x/y anchor point set to their top-left corner, so that means your new circleSprite also has its anchor point at the top-left corner.

Drawing on a Single Graphics Context

In the previous examples, we created a new Graphics object for each line and shape that we wanted to make. This is fine, if you're making a small number of shapes (say, a few hundred), but if you are making thousands, there's a more computationally efficient way to do it: *draw all your shapes on a single* **graphics context**. *Graphics context* is a formal term for describing the Graphics object onto which we've been drawing our shapes and lines.

Here's some sample code to illustrate this. (In this code, "ctx" stands for "context.")

```
//Create a single graphics context
let ctx = new Graphics();

//Draw a rectangle on the graphics context
ctx.beginFill(0x0033CC);
ctx.lineStyle(4, 0xFF0000, 1);
ctx.drawRect(32, 32, 96, 96);
ctx.endFill();

//Draw a circle without an outline
ctx.beginFill(0xFF9933);
ctx.lineStyle(0);
ctx.drawCircle(224, 80, 48);
ctx.endFill();

//Draw a line
ctx.lineStyle(4, 0x000000, 1);
ctx.moveTo(320, 48);
ctx.lineTo(420, 112);

//Add the graphics context to the stage
stage.addChild(ctx);
```

Figure 3-12 illustrates what this code produces.

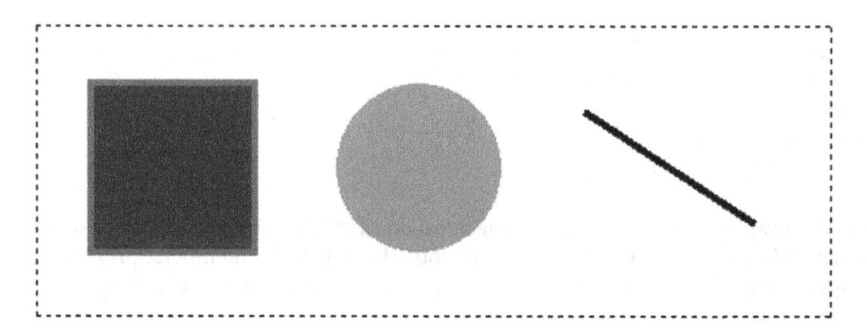

Figure 3-12. *Drawing shapes on a single graphics context for optimized rendering*

Notice that the x/y positions of the lines and shapes are relative to the graphics context's top-left corner. The graphics context itself is at position 0,0 on the canvas.

Another important detail in the preceding code is that if you want to draw a shape without an outline, set the lineStyle to 0 before you draw the shape, as follows:

```
ctx.lineStyle(0);
```

Give lineStyle new values if you want to draw another line on the same graphics context.

Redrawing Animated Graphics Each Frame

At some point, you might have to animate lines and shapes in your application. There are two ways to do this.

The easy way is to just create a shape from a single Graphics object and change its x/y position inside a game loop, just as we animated sprites in the previous chapter. That might be all you need. But if you want to animate the length of a line, the curve of an arc, or the corners of a rectangle, you'll need to redraw that shape each frame.

A practical example is the best way to see how to do this. Run the animatingGraphics.html file located in the chapter's source code, for a dynamically animated line in action (illustrated in Figure 3-13). The two ends of the line turn continuously around invisible points in space. The effect is like a crankshaft turning an invisible wheel, or a line buffeted by eddies of air or water. It's fun to watch—and even slightly spooky.

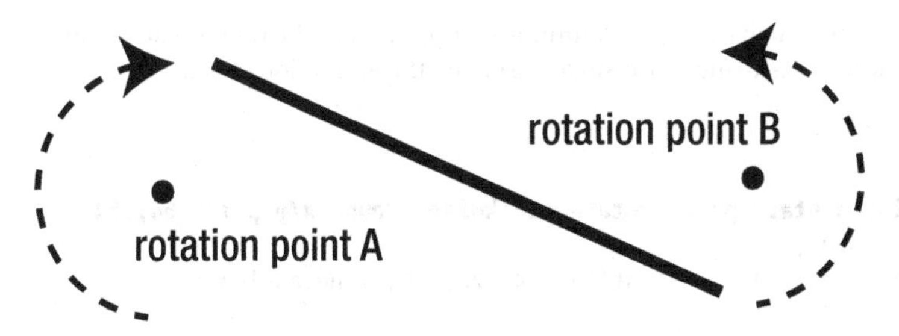

Figure 3-13. *A dynamically animated line*

The effect works with the help of a custom function called `rotateAroundPoint`.

```
function rotateAroundPoint(pointX, pointY, distanceX, distanceY, angle) {
 let point = {};
 point.x = pointX + Math.cos(angle) * distanceX;
 point.y = pointY + Math.sin(angle) * distanceY;
 return point;
}
```

The `rotateAroundPoint` function returns a `point` object with `x` and `y` values that represent the axis of rotation. The `distanceX` and `distanceY` arguments define the radius from the center of rotation to the edge of the imaginary circle that's being traced in space. If `distanceX` and `distanceY` have the same values, the function will trace a circle. If you give them different values, the function will trace an ellipse. You can use the `point` object that `rotatePoint` returns to make any other `x/y` point rotate around that axis.

Here's the code that uses `rotateAroundPoint` to create the wobbly line effect shown in Figure 3-13. The `setup` function creates the line and adds two properties to it: `angleA` and `angleB`, both initialized to zero. These new properties will be used to help update the angle of rotation on the line's start and end points.

```
let line;

function setup() {

  //Create the line
  line = new Graphics();
  stage.addChild(line);

  //Add `angleA` and `angleB` properties
  line.angleA = 0;
  line.angleB = 0;

  //Start the game loop
  gameLoop();
}
```

The play function (which runs in a continuous loop) updates the rotation angles and redraws the line each frame, using those angles to create the animation effect.

```
function play() {

  //Make the line's start point rotate clockwise around x/y point 64, 64
  line.angleA += 0.02;
  let rotatingA = rotateAroundPoint(64, 64, 20, 20, line.angleA);

  //Make the line's end point rotate counter-clockwise
  //around x/y point 192, 208
  line.angleB -= 0.03;
  let rotatingB = rotateAroundPoint(192, 208, 20, 20, line.angleB);

  //Clear the line to reset it from the previous frame
  line.clear();

  //Draw the line using the rotating points as start and end points
  line.lineStyle(4, 0x000000, 1);
  line.moveTo(rotatingA.x, rotatingA.y);
  line.lineTo(rotatingB.x, rotatingB.y);
}
```

The most important thing to note is that, before the line is drawn, the clear method runs (clear is a method on all Graphics objects).

```
line.clear();
```

This erases the line that was drawn in the previous frame. It means that the line that is drawn in the current frame will be using the updated start and end points. This is what creates the animation effect. Without using clear, the lines drawn in previous frames would remain on the canvas, producing a ghost-trail effect, something such as what you can see in Figure 3-14. This could be a desirable effect in some situations, however, so keep that in mind!

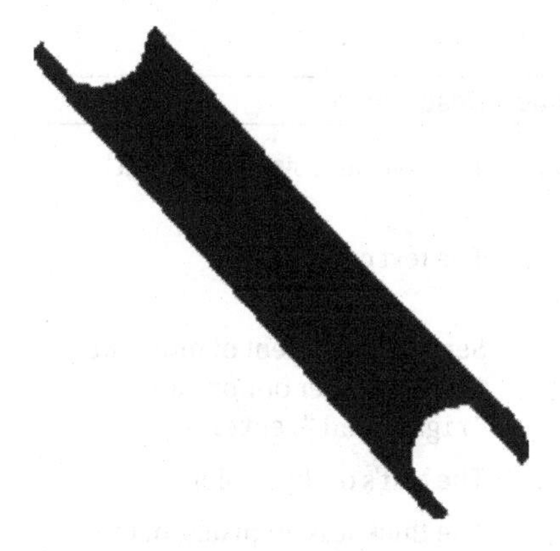

Figure 3-14. If you don't clear the graphics from the previous frame, the new line will be drawn on top of the old lines

Now that you know all about how to draw lines and shapes, let's find out how to display text.

Displaying Text

Pixi gives you two basic ways to display text. You can either display text using an ordinary font file (with a TTF, OTF, TTC, or WOFF extension). Or, you could use a special bitmap font (with an XML or FNT extension). There are advantages and disadvantages to both approaches, so let's find out what they are.

The Text Object

The easiest way to display text with Pixi is to use the `Text` object (`PIXI.Text`). The constructor takes two arguments: the text you want to display and a style object that defines the font's properties.

```
message = new Text(
  "Hello Pixi!",
  {font: "48px Impact", fill: "red"}
);
```

The style object (the second argument) can be supplied with a huge number of optional properties. Table 3-1 shows the complete list of style options from Pixi's documentation.

Table 3-1. *Style Options*

Name	Value Type	Default Value	Description
font	String	"bold 20px Arial"	The style and size of the font
fill	String or number	"black"	The text color
align	String	"left"	Sets the alignment of multiline text. The other options are "right" and "center".
stroke	String	None	The text's outline color
strokeThickness	Number	0	The thickness, in pixels, of the text outline
wordWrap	Boolean (true/false)	false	Sets word-wrapping for multiline text
wordWrapWidth	Number	100	Width at which word-wrapping will start to occur. (wordWrap must also be set to true.)
lineHeight	Number	None	The vertical space used by the text
dropShadow	Boolean	false	Sets a drop shadow effect
dropShadowColor	String	"#000000"	The shadow's color
dropShadowAngle	Number	Math.PI/4	The shadow's angle
dropShadowDistance	Number	5	This size of the shadow, in pixels
padding	Number	0	Adds padding to the top and bottom of fonts. This is to help prevent unwanted cropping that occurs with some fonts.
textBaseLine	String	"alphabetic"	The baseline on which the text is drawn. Other options are "top", "hanging", "middle", "ideographic", and "bottom".
lineJoin	String	"mitre"	The corner style of the text. Changing lineJoin can fix problems with spiky text. The two other options are "round" and "bevel".
mitreLimit	Number	10	The limit, if you're using the "mitre" lineJoin option. This can reduce or increase text spikiness.

■ **Note** All text colors can be in either RGBA, HLSA, Hex, or HTML color strings, such as "blue" or "green." Pixi makes text objects by using the Canvas drawing API to render the text to an invisible and temporary canvas element. It then turns the canvas into a WebGL texture, so that it can be mapped onto a sprite. That's why the text's color has to be wrapped in a string: it's a Canvas drawing API color value.

Pixi's `Text` objects are inherited from the `Sprite` class, so they contain all the same properties, such as `x`, `y`, `width`, `height`, `alpha`, `rotation`, and all the rest. Position and resize them just as you would any other sprite. Following is how you could center some text inside the canvas. Figure 3-15 shows how this appears.

```
message.x = renderer.view.width / 2 - message.width / 2;
message.y = renderer.view.height / 2 - message.height / 2;
```

***Figure 3-15.** Using a `Text` object to render text*

And, just like any other sprite, you have to add text to the `stage` object before it's visible on the canvas.

```
stage.addChild(message);
```

If you want to change the message content, use the `text` method, and set it to any string you want to display, such as the following:

```
message.text = "Text changed!";
```

Use the `style` property to redefine the font properties, as follows:

```
message.style = ({fill: "black", font: "16px Helvetica"});
```

Pixi can also wrap long lines of text. Set the text's `wordWrap` style property to `true`, and then set `wordWrapWidth` to the maximum length, in pixels, that the line of text should be.

```
message.style = ({wordWrap: true, wordWrapWidth: 100});
```

So far in these examples, the code has only used built-in system fonts, such as Impact and Helvetica. But what if you want to load and use a custom TTF, OTF, or WOFF font file?

Loading Font Files

Loading font files poses a particular problem, because, unlike images, there's no built-in HTML5 API to force them to load before they can be used. And Pixi doesn't have any built-in solutions for this. The best you can do is link to the font file that you want to use with the help of the CSS `@font-face` rule. Here's how:

```
@font-face {
 font-family: "fontFamilyName";
 src: url("fonts/fontFile.ttf");
}
```

You can either write this code into your HTML document by hand or, better yet, use a JavaScript function to do it for you. Here's one called `linkFont` that does the trick:

```
function linkFont(source) {

  //Use the font's filename as the `fontFamily` name. This code captures
  //the font file's name without the extension or file path
  let fontFamily = source.split("/").pop().split(".")[0];
```

```
  //Append an `@afont-face` style rule to the head of the HTML document
  let newStyle = document.createElement("style");
  let fontFace
    = "@font-face {font-family: '" + fontFamily
    + "'; src: url('" + source + "');}";
  newStyle.appendChild(document.createTextNode(fontFace));
  document.head.appendChild(newStyle);
}
```

Use this function by passing it a string of the file path for the font you want to load, as follows:

```
linkFont("fonts/anyFont.ttf");
```

`linkFont` just dynamically writes the preceding CSS code based on the file path of the font. Use `linkFont` after you load other images or JSON files, using Pixi's `loader`, like this:

```
loader
  .add("images/anyImage")
  .load(setup);

linkFont("fonts/SpicyRice.ttf");
linkFont("fonts/puzzler.otf");
```

But here's the problem: the CSS code that `linkFont` produces doesn't actually load the font; it just tells the browser where to find it. All browsers will only download the fonts when they're used on the page, and never before. This means that anyone using your application might see a brief flash of un-styled text before the font is loaded. Or, the font just won't load. And, unfortunately, at the time of writing, there's no new HTML5 spec on the horizon to help solve this.

But that's OK; we've got a workaround! The reason is because all your Pixi games and applications will be running in a game loop. So, just set your `Text` objects to a font you want to load *inside the game loop*. In the application structure we've been using, you would do it in the `play` function, as follows:

```
function play() {
  message.style = {font: "16px theFontFamilyName"};
}
```

This guarantees that the browser will have loaded the font file by the time the style is applied.

■ **Note** Don't despair! For the ultimate fix, use a brilliant font preloader called `Font.js` (`github.com/Pomax/Font.js`). It uses some sneaky coding to trick the browser into loading the font file before it's displayed on the HTML page or canvas. `Font.js` is great, so use it! At the time of writing, the Pixi development team was also thinking of building a similar font preloader into Pixi's loader. Check—it might be there by the time you're reading this.

Using Bitmap Fonts

Because of all the quirkiness and inconsistencies of working with font files, Pixi gives you another more reliable way of displaying custom fonts: bitmap fonts. Bitmap fonts are just sets of images. They contain an image for each character of the alphabet in the font set. So, instead of using the browser to render the shape of the letter, an image of the letter is displayed instead. This is great, because you have a total guarantee that the font will display exactly as you expect it to.

■ **Note** A possible disadvantage to bitmap fonts is that, because they're just images, they have to be loaded like images and will also use more memory than vector-based TTF and OTF font files. However, that also makes them more CPU efficient, because, unlike vector-based files, the font outlines don't have to be drawn dynamically by the CPU. So, overall, you might get marginally better performance by using bitmap fonts.

Before you can use a bitmap font in Pixi, you have to create it. Fortunately, there are plenty of good software tools to help you do this, including the popular Glyph Designer. (Do a web search to locate the URL of its current home page.) They all work pretty much the same way: you load up an ordinary TTF or OTF font file, set some options, and get back a texture atlas of images for each letter shape. Figure 3-16 shows a free online tool called Littera (`www.kvazars.com`) that helps you do this.

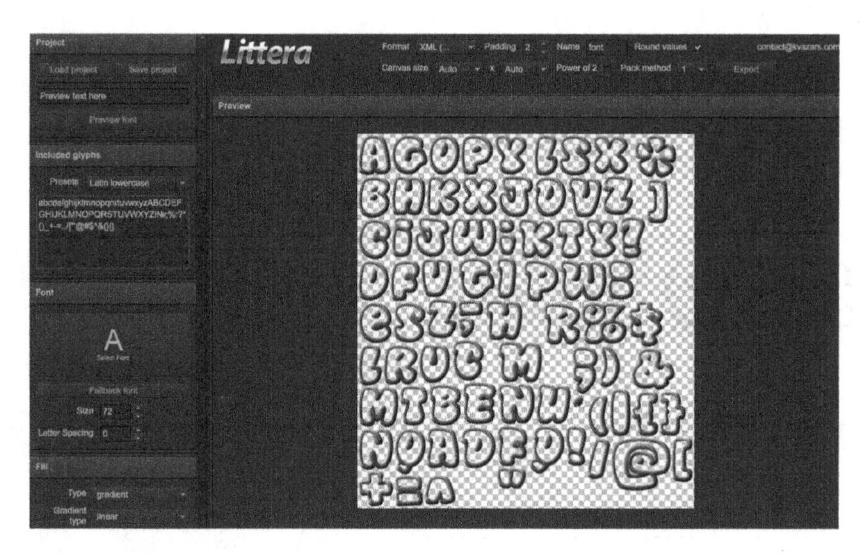

Figure 3-16. *Creating a bitmap font*

Does that look familiar? Yes, you're right; it's just a texture atlas made up of letter-shaped images, just like the texture atlas you learned to use in Chapter 1. The texture atlas is made up of two files: a PNG file containing the images and a matching XML data file (often using a `.fnt` file extension) that describes the position of each letter image in the PNG file.

When you've got those files, copy them both into your project's fonts folder, and use Pixi's loader to load the XML file.

```
loader
  .add("fonts/disko.xml")
  .load(setup);
```

Next, use the `BitmapText` class (`PIXI.extras.BitmapText`) to create the text.

```
message = new BitmapText(
  "Hello Pixi!",
  {font: "48px disko"}
);
```

Figure 3-17 shows an example of what this code produces.

Figure 3-17. Displaying the bitmap text

■ **Note** If you have any trouble loading the font or creating the `BitmapText` object, open the XML file in a text editor and make sure that the name of the font face property matches the name of the font you want to load. Also, make sure the file property matches the name of PNG file that contains the letter images.

You can display the font in any size you like: 48px, 16px, 12px, or whatever. The letter images will scale to the right size.

`BitmapText` objects share all the same properties as Pixi's sprites, but they have only the following three font options you can set:

- **`font`**: The font size and name
- **`align`**: The alignment for multiline text: `"left"`, `"right"`, or `"center"`
- **`tint`**: The tint color of the text: any RGBA, HLASA, Hex, or HTML string color value

This might seem limited, but it's all you need. That's because, if you're working with bitmap fonts, all the customization and tweaking of the font style occurs in the software you use to create the font texture atlas.

We're now finished with shapes and text! The last part of this chapter covers something quite different, but it's an essential skill that you need to have.

Grouping Sprites

It's sometimes useful to be able to group sprites, text, and shapes together. You can group things together to make compound objects or use groups to organize sprites into different game scenes or for different display screens in your application. Pixi gives you two ways to make groups: using a `Container` object or using a high-performance `ParticleContainer`.

Using a Container

A practical example is the best way to learn how to group sprites using a `Container`. Imagine that you want to display three sprites: a cat, hedgehog, and tiger. Create them and set their positions—*but don't add them to the stage.*

```
//The cat
cat = new Sprite(id["cat.png"]);
cat.position.set(0, 0);

//The hedgehog
hedgehog = new Sprite(id["hedgehog.png"]);
hedgehog.position.set(32, 32);

//The tiger
tiger = new Sprite(id["tiger.png"]);
tiger.position.set(64, 64);
```

Next, create a `Container` (`PIXI.Container`) called `animals` to group them together, like this:

```
animals = new Container();
```

Then use `addChild` to add the sprites to the `animals` group.

```
animals.addChild(cat);
animals.addChild(hedgehog);
animals.addChild(tiger);
```

Finally, add the `animals` group to the stage.

```
stage.addChild(animals);
```

Figure 3-18 shows what this code produces. What you can't see on Pixi's canvas is that there's an invisible box, called `animals`, that's grouping all the sprites together.

Figure 3-18. Grouping the sprites

You can now treat the `animals` group as a single unit. You can think of a `Container` as a special kind of sprite that doesn't have a texture. If you need a list of all the child sprites that `animals` contains, use its `children` array to obtain one.

```
console.log(animals.chidren)
//Displays: Array [Object, Object, Object]
```

This tells you that `animals` has three sprites as children.

Because the `animals` group is just like any other sprite, you can change its `x` and `y` values, `alpha`, `scale`, and all the other sprite properties. For example, if you want to find out the dimensions of the group, the `width` and `height` properties will tell you, as shown in Figure 3-19.

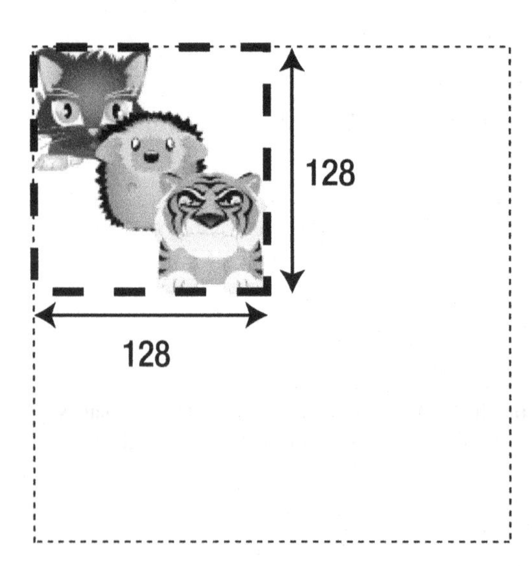

Figure 3-19. The size of the group matches its contents

The width and height of the group are determined by the size of the sprites that it contains.

```
console.log(`Width: ${animals.width} Height: ${animals.height}`);
//Displays: 128, 128
```

Any property value you change on the parent container will affect the child sprites in a relative way. What happens if you change a group's width or height?

```
animals.width = 200;
animals.height = 200;
```

The child sprites rescale relative to the new size, as shown in Figure 3-20.

Figure 3-20. *Changing the container's size scales its contents*

If you set the group's x and y position, all the child sprites will be repositioned relative to the group's top-left corner. What would happen if you set the group's x and y positions to 96?

```
animals.position.set(96, 96);
```

Figure 3-21 shows the effect: the entire group of sprites will move 96 pixels right and 96 pixels down.

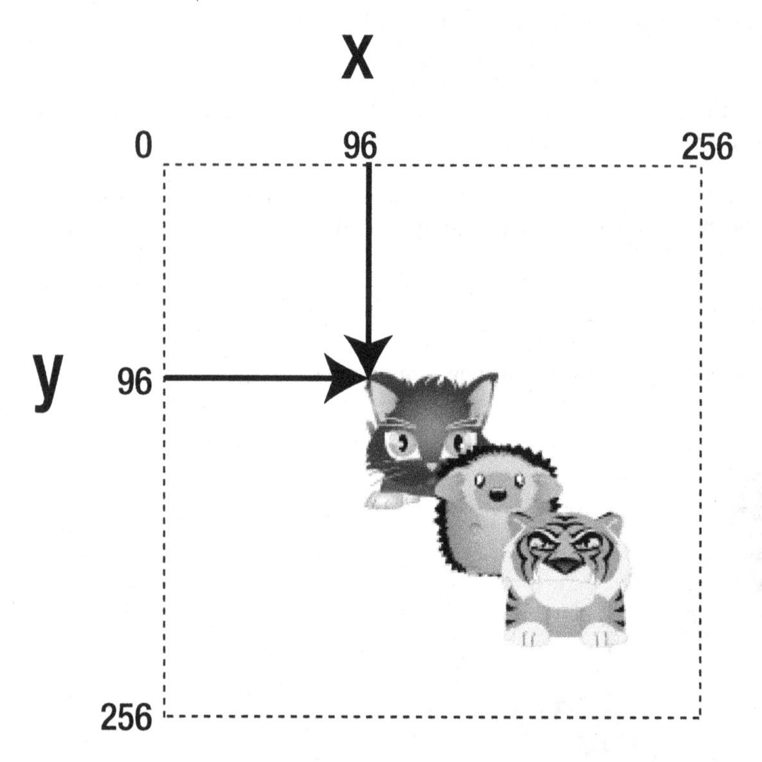

Figure 3-21. Moving the group by setting its x and y positions

You can nest as many `Container` objects inside other `Container` objects as you like, to create complex hierarchies, if you need to. However, a Pixi `DisplayObject` (such as a `Sprite` or another `Container`) can only belong to one parent at a time. If you use `addChild` to make a sprite the child of another object, Pixi will automatically remove it from its current parent. That's a useful bit of management that you don't have to worry about.

■ **Note** A hierarchy of sprites organized into nested parent-child containers like this is called a **scene graph**.

Local and Global Positions

When you add a sprite to a `Container`, its x and y positions are *relative to the group's top-left corner*. That's the sprite's local position. For example, what do you think the tiger's local position is in Figure 3-21? Let's find out.

```
console.log(`Tiger local x: ${tiger.x}`);
console.log(`Tiger local y: ${tiger.y}`);
//Displays:
//Tiger local x: 64
//Tiger local y: 64
```

This tells us that the tiger is at an x position of 64, and a y position of 64, relative to the top-left corner of the animals group. Figure 3-22 illustrates this.

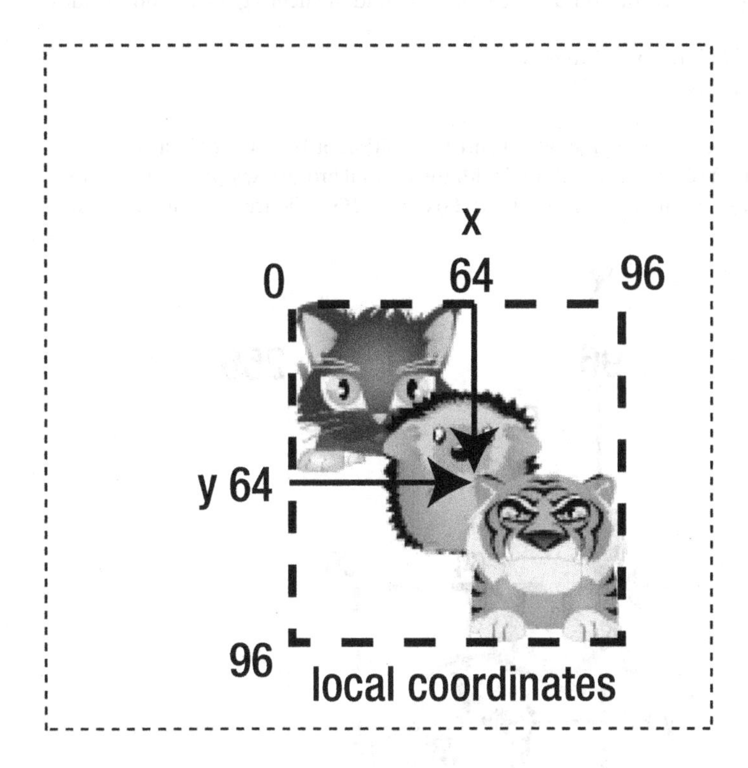

Figure 3-22. The tiger's x and y positions are relative to the group

Sprites also have a global position. The global position is the distance from the top-left corner of the root container (usually the stage) to the sprite's anchor point (usually the sprite's top-left corner). You can find a sprite's global position with the help of the `toGlobal` method. Here's the format you need to use it:

```
parentSprite.toGlobal(childSprite.position)
```

The `toGlobal` method returns an object with x and y properties that tell you the sprite's global position. Here's how you could use `toGlobal` to find the tiger's global x and y values:

```
animals.toGlobal(tiger.position).x
animals.toGlobal(tiger.position).y
```

This will give you an x position of 160 and a y position of 160. Why? Because the tiger's local x/y point (64, 64) is combined with the animal group's x/y point (96, 96) to give you a global x/y point of 160, 160 (64 plus 96 equals 160). Figure 3-23 illustrates this.

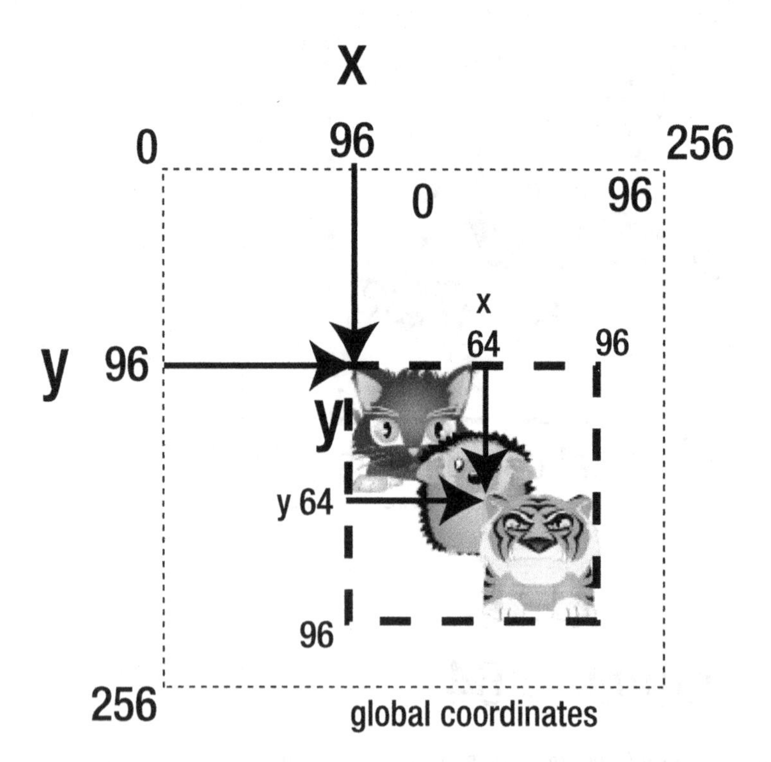

animals.toGlobal(tiger.position).x = 160
animals.toGlobal(tiger.position).y = 160

Figure 3-23. *Using toGlobal to find a sprite's global position*

What if you want to find the global position of a sprite but don't know what the sprite's parent container is? Every sprite has a property called `parent` that will tell you what the sprite's parent is. If you add a sprite directly to the `stage` container, `stage` will be the sprite's parent. In the preceding example, the tiger's parent is `animals`. That means you can alternatively get the tiger's global position by writing code such as this:

```
tiger.parent.toGlobal(tiger.position);
```

And it will work even if you don't know what the tiger's parent container currently is.

There's one more way to calculate the global position! If you want to know the distance from the top-left corner of the canvas to the sprite, and don't know or care what the sprite's parent containers are, use the `getGlobalPosition` method. Here's how to use it to find the tiger's global position:

```
tiger.getGlobalPosition().x
tiger.getGlobalPosition().y
```

The special thing about `getGlobalPosition` is that it's highly precise: it will give you the sprite's accurate global position at the *exact instant* its local position changes. The other ways of calculating global position give you a number that's usually one frame behind, if you calculate them inside the game loop. I asked the Pixi development team to add this feature specifically for accurate collision detection for games, and you'll see in Chapter 7 how useful it will be.

What if you want to convert a global position to a local position? You can use the `toLocal` method. It works in a similar way but uses the following general format:

```
sprite.toLocal(sprite.position, anyOtherSprite)
```

Use `toLocal` to determine the distance between a sprite and any other sprite. Here's how you could find out the tiger's local position, relative to the hedgehog.

```
tiger.toLocal(tiger.position, hedgehog).x
tiger.toLocal(tiger.position, hedgehog).y
```

This gives you an `x` value of 32 and a `y` value of 32. You can see in the sample images that the tiger's top-left corner is 32 pixels down and to the left of the hedgehog's top-left corner.

Using a ParticleContainer

Pixi has an alternative, high-performance way to group sprites, called a `ParticleContainer` (`PIXI.ParticleContainer`). Any sprites inside a `ParticleContainer` will render two to five times faster than they would if they were in a regular `Container`. It's a great performance boost for games.

Create a ParticleContainer like this:

```
let superFastSprites = new ParticleContainer();
```

Then use addChild to add sprites to it, just as you would with any ordinary Container.

You have to make some compromises if you decide to use a ParticleContainer. Sprites inside the ParticleContainer can only use a few basic properties: x, y, width, height, scale, alpha, pivot, and visible—and that's about it. Also, the sprites that it contains can't have nested children of their own. A ParticleContainer also can't use Pixi's advanced visual effects, such as filters, masks, and blend modes (which you'll learn all about in Chapter 6). But for the huge performance boost that you get, those compromises are usually worth it. And you can use Containers and ParticleContainers simultaneously in the same project, so you can fine-tune your optimization.

■ **Note** Why are sprites in a ParticleContainer so fast? Because the positions of the sprites are being calculated directly on the GPU.

Where you create a ParticleContainer, there are two optional arguments you can provide: the maximum number of sprites the container can hold and an options object.

```
let superFastSprites = new ParticleContainer(size, options);
```

The default value for size is 15,000. So, if you have to contain more sprites, set it to a higher number. The options argument is an object with five Boolean properties that you can set: scale, position, rotation, alpha, and uvs. The default value for position is true, but all the others are set to false. That means that if you want to change the rotation, scale, or alpha of a sprite in the ParticleContainer, you have to set those properties to true, as follows:

```
let superFastSprites = new ParticleContainer(
  size,
  {
    rotation: true,
    alpha: true,
    scale: true,
    uvs: true
  }
);
```

But, if you don't think you'll have to use these properties, keep them set to false, to squeeze out the maximum amount of performance.

Hey, what is `uvs`? `u` and `v` are the WebGL terms for normalized `x` and `y` texture position values. They refer to the `x` and `y` positions of the section of the texture you want to display as a normalized (0 to 1) value. What that means is that if you are using different sub-images from a spritesheet to create your particles, the different particles will have different `uvs`, so you will have to set it to `true`.

■ **Note** Why doesn't WebGL just use `x` and `y` instead of `u` an `v`? Because the WebGL specification reserved the names `x` and `y` for something else!

Summary

In this chapter, you've learned all the basic skills you need to know to start creating interactive images with Pixi. You've learned how to make basic shapes, such as rectangles, circles, and lines, and how to animate shapes dynamically inside a game loop. You now also know how to load font files, create bitmap fonts, and use those fonts to display text. You've also found out everything you need to know about the local and global positions of sprites and shapes and how to group sprites together using `Containers` and Pixi's high-performance `ParticleContainers`.

You've now got all the basic tools to start using Pixi to make some really fun stuff. But what can you make? In the next chapter, you'll find out: we're going to make a simple game using all the skills you've learned so far.

CHAPTER 4

Making Games

I've covered all the basics of working with Pixi, so we can now start making some fun stuff! Games are a great place to start, because they give you a chance to practice all the skills you've learned so far, and games are a great model for interactive applications of all kinds. Making a game will also give you a chance to learn an essential new skill: how to check if two sprites are touching, and what to do when they are.

In this chapter, you're going to learn how to make a basic game prototype called Treasure Hunter. It's the most basic complete game you can make but contains all the essentials you need to know to make much bigger games. Here's what you'll learn in this chapter:

- Collision detection: how to check if two sprites are touching
- Making enemy sprites with simple artificial intelligence
- Different game scenes and how to switch between scenes to control the flow of a game
- Single compound sprites made up of different sub-sprites
- Game logic: how to determine if a player has won or lost the game

At the end of this chapter, you'll be well on your way to start making your own original games.

Collision Detection

You now know how to make a huge variety of graphics objects, but what can you do with them? A fun thing to do is to build a simple **collision detection** system. Pixi doesn't have a built-in collision detection system, but I wrote an easy-to-use library called Bump.js that gives you all the collision tools you'll need to make most kinds of 2D action games. Let's find out how to install and set up Bump, and then how to use it to make a game.

Installing and Setting Up Bump

First, download Bump from its code repository: github.com/kittykatattack/bump. Next, use a <script> tag to link the bump.js file to your HTML document. Here's how the bump.js file is linked to the HTML document in the sample files that you'll find in this chapter's source code:

```
<script src="../library/bump/bin/bump.js"></script>
```

(If you prefer, you can load bump.js using any JavaScript module system you might be familiar working with: ES6 modules, SystemJS, AMD, or CommonJS.)

Finally, in your setup function, create a new instance of Bump, like this:

```
b = new Bump(PIXI);
```

The variable b (for *bump*, of course!) now represents the running instance of Bump that you can use to access all of Bump's collision methods.

Using the hitTestRectangle Method

Bump has a whole suite of built-in collision methods that you can use for games, but in this book, we only need to use one: hitTestRectangle. (Refer to Bump's source code repository for details on how to use the other methods.) hitTestRectangle checks whether any two rectangular sprites are touching.

```
b.hitTestRectangle(spriteOne, spriteTwo)
```

If they overlap, hitTestRectangle will return true. You can use hitTestRectangle with an if statement, to check for a collision between two sprites, like this:

```
if (b.hitTestRectangle(cat, box)) {
  //There's a collision
} else {
  //There's no collision
}
```

As you'll soon see, hitTestRectangle is your front door into the vast universe of game design.

Collision Detection in Action

Run the rectangleCollision.html file in the chapter's source files for a working example of how to use hitTestRectangle. Use the arrow keys to move the cat sprite. If the cat hits the box, the box becomes red, and "hit!" is displayed by the text object. Figure 4-1 illustrates how the sample program runs.

Figure 4-1. *Using collision detection to find out if the cat and the box are touching*

You've already seen all the code that creates all these elements, as well as the keyboard control system that makes the cat move. The only new thing remaining is the way `hitTestRectangle` is used inside the `play` function to check for a collision.

```
function play() {

  //Apply the velocity values to the sprite's position to make it move
  cat.x += cat.vx;
  cat.y += cat.vy;

  //check for a collision between the cat and the box
  if (hitTestRectangle(cat, box)) {

    //if there's a collision, change the message text and tint the box red
    message.text = "hit!";
    box.tint = 0xFF3300;
  } else {

    //if there's no collision, reset the message text and the box's color
    message.text = "No collision...";
    box.tint = 0xFFFFFF;
  }
}
```

You know from Chapters 2 and 3 that the `play` function is being called by the game loop 60 times per second, which means that the `if` statement in the preceding code is also constantly checking for a collision between the cat and the box 60 times per second. If `hitTestRectangle` is `true`, the text `message` object sets its `text` to `"hit"`, as follows:

```
message.text = "hit";
```

The color of the box is tinted red by setting the box's `tint` property to the hexadecimal red value.

```
box.tint = 0xff3300;
```

■ **Note** All sprites have a `tint` property that you can use to colorize them in a particular way.

If there's no collision, the message and box are maintained in their original states.

```
message.setText("No collision...");
box.tint = 0xccff99;
```

This code is pretty simple, but suddenly you've created an interactive world that seems to be completely alive. It's almost like magic! And, perhaps surprisingly, you now have all the skills you need to start making games with Pixi!

■ **Note** How does the `hitTestRectangle` method actually work under the hood? See *Advanced Game Design with HTML5 and JavaScript* (Apress, 2015) for a detailed explanation.

Treasure Hunter

I told you that you now have all the skills you need to start making games. What? You don't believe me? Let me prove it to you! Let's take a closer look at how to make an object-collection-and-enemy-avoidance game called Treasure Hunter, as shown in Figure 4-2. (You'll find the complete game in this chapter's source files.)

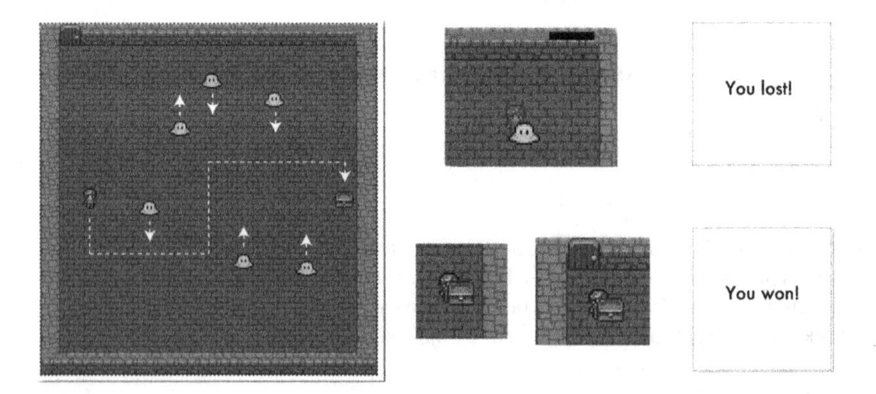

Figure 4-2. *Collecting the treasure, avoiding the blob monsters, and reaching the exit*

Treasure Hunter is a good example of one of simplest complete games you can make using the tools you've learned so far. Use the keyboard arrow keys to help the explorer find the treasure and carry it to the exit. Six blob monsters move up and down between the dungeon walls, and if they hit the explorer, he becomes semitransparent, and the health meter at the top right corner shrinks. If all the health is used up, "You lost!" is displayed on the canvas; if the explorer reaches the exit with the treasure, "You won!" is displayed. Although it's a basic prototype, Treasure Hunter contains most of the elements you'll find in much bigger games: texture atlas graphics, interactivity, collision, and multiple game scenes. Let's go on a tour of how the game was put together, so that you can use it as a starting point for one of your own games.

The Code Structure

Open the `treasureHunter.js` file, and you'll see that all the game code is in one big file. Here's a bird's-eye view of how all the code is organized:

```
//Set up Pixi and load the texture atlas files - call the `setup`
//function when they've loaded

//Declare any variables used in more than one function

function setup() {

  //Initialize the game sprites, set the game `state` to `play`
  //and start the 'gameLoop'
}

function gameLoop() {

  //Runs the current game `state` in a loop and render the sprites
}

function play() {

  //All the game logic goes here
}

function end() {

  //All the code that should run at the end of the game goes here
}

//The game's helper functions:
//`keyboard`, `hitTestRectangle`, `contain` and `randomInt`
```

Use this as your world map of the complete code, as we look at how each section ahead works. You already know the details of this code structure from the many examples in Chapters 2 and 3, so I'll only be highlighting the new parts in the code samples that follow. Refer back to earlier examples, or the complete code in this chapter's source files, for a reminder of the complete picture.

Initialize the Game in the Setup Function

As soon as the texture atlas images have loaded, the `setup` function runs. It only runs once, and lets you perform one-time setup tasks for your game. It's a great place to create and initialize objects, sprites, game scenes, populate data arrays, or parse loaded JSON game data.

Here's an abridged view of the `setup` function in Treasure Hunter and the tasks that it performs.

```
function setup() {

  //Create a new instance of the Bump collision library
  //Create an `id` alias for the texture atlas frame ids

  //The `gameScene` container that contains all the main
  //game sprites

  //Create the main sprites:
  //The `dungeon` sprite
  //The `door` sprite
  //The `explorer` sprite
  //The `treasure` sprite
  //The `blobs` enemy sprites

  //Create the `healthBar` compound sprite

  //Add some text for the game over message

  //Create a `gameOverScene` container to contain the text
  //that will be displayed when the game is finished

  //Assign the player's keyboard controllers

  //set the game state to `play`
  state = play;

  //Start the game loop
  gameLoop();
}
```

The last two lines of code in the preceding setup function are perhaps the most important.

```
state = play;
gameLoop();
```

Running gameLoop switches on the game's engine, and causes the play function to be called in a continuous loop. But before we look at how that works, let's see what the specific code inside the setup function does.

Creating the Game Scenes

The setup function creates two Container groups called gameScene and gameOverScene. Each of these is added to the stage.

```
gameScene = new Container();
stage.addChild(gameScene);
gameOverScene = new Container();
stage.addChild(gameOverScene);
```

All of the sprites that are part of the main game are added to the gameScene group. The "game over" text message that should be displayed at the end of the game is added to the gameOverScene group. (See Figure 4-3.)

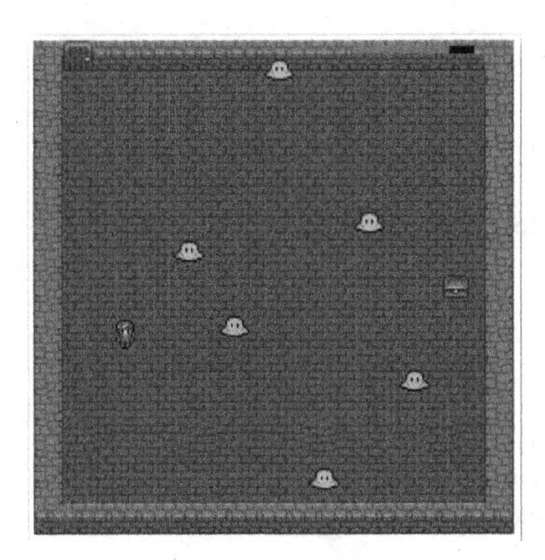

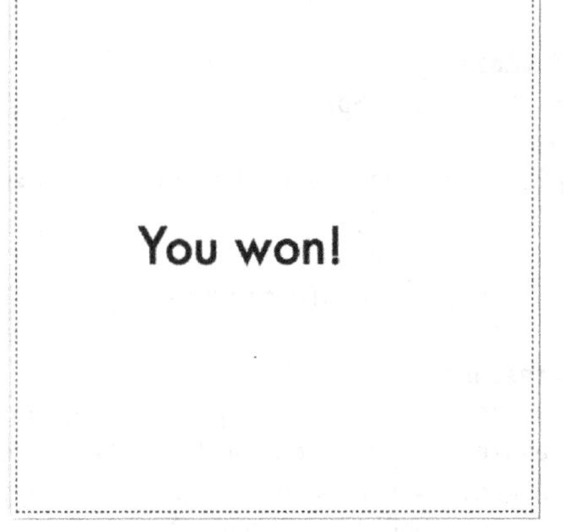

Figure 4-3. The game's two scenes

Although it's created in the setup function, gameOverScene shouldn't be visible when the game first starts, so its visible property is initialized to false.

```
gameOverScene.visible = false;
```

You'll see ahead that, when the game ends, the gameOverScene's visible property will be set to true, to display the text that appears at the end of the game.

You can think of game scenes as pages in a book. Treasure Hunter just has two pages, but most games will have many more. Just add as many additional scenes (pages) as you need for your own games, and you can create games of great complexity, using this same basic model.

Making the Dungeon, Door, Explorer, and Treasure

The dungeon background, exit door, explorer (player), and treasure chest images are all sprites made from texture atlas frames. Most important, they're all added as children of the gameScene.

```
//Dungeon
dungeon = new Sprite(id["dungeon.png"]);
gameScene.addChild(dungeon);

//Door
door = new Sprite(id["door.png"]);
door.position.set(32, 0);
gameScene.addChild(door);

//Explorer
explorer = new Sprite(id["explorer.png"]);
explorer.x = 68;
explorer.y = gameScene.height / 2 - explorer.height / 2;
explorer.vx = 0;
explorer.vy = 0;
gameScene.addChild(explorer);

//Treasure
treasure = new Sprite(id["treasure.png"]);
treasure.x = gameScene.width - treasure.width - 48;
treasure.y = gameScene.height / 2 - treasure.height / 2;
gameScene.addChild(treasure);
```

Keeping them together in the gameScene group will make it easy for us to hide the gameScene and display the gameOverScene when the game is finished.

Making the Blob Monsters

The six blob monsters are created in a loop. Each blob is given a random initial position and velocity. The vertical velocity is alternately multiplied by 1 or -1 for each blob, and that's what causes each blob to move in the direction opposite to the one next to it. Each blob monster that's created is pushed into an array called blobs.

```
let numberOfBlobs = 6,
    spacing = 48,
    xOffset = 150,
    speed = 2,
    direction = 1;

//An array to store all the blob monsters
blobs = [];

//Make as many blobs as there are `numberOfBlobs`
for (let i = 0; i < numberOfBlobs; i++) {

  //Make a blob
  let blob = new Sprite(id["blob.png"]);

  //Space each blob horizontally according to the `spacing` value.
  //`xOffset` determines the point from the left of the screen
  //at which the first blob should be added
  let x = spacing * i + xOffset;

  //Give the blob a random y position
  let y = randomInt(0, stage.height - blob.height);

  //Set the blob's position
  blob.x = x;
  blob.y = y;

  //Set the blob's vertical velocity. `direction` will be either `1` or
  //`-1`. `1` means the enemy will move down and `-1` means the blob will
  //move up. Multiplying `direction` by `speed` determines the blob's
  //vertical direction
  blob.vy = speed * direction;

  //Reverse the direction for the next blob
  direction *= -1;

  //Push the blob into the `blobs` array
  blobs.push(blob);

  //Add the blob to the `gameScene`
  gameScene.addChild(blob);
}
```

Making the Health Bar

When you play Treasure Hunter, you'll notice that when the explorer touches one of the enemies, the width of the health bar at the top right corner of the screen decreases. How was this health bar made? It's just two overlapping rectangles at exactly the same position: a black rectangle behind, and a red rectangle in front. They're grouped into a single `healthBar` group. The `healthBar` group is then added to gameScene and positioned on the stage.

```
//Create the container
healthBar = new Container();
healthBar.position.set(stage.width - 170, 4);
gameScene.addChild(healthBar);

//Create the black background rectangle
let innerBar = new Graphics();
innerBar.beginFill(0x000000);
innerBar.drawRect(0, 0, 128, 8);
innerBar.endFill();
healthBar.addChild(innerBar);

//Create the front red rectangle
let outerBar = new Graphics();
outerBar.beginFill(0xFF3300);
outerBar.drawRect(0, 0, 128, 8);
outerBar.endFill();
healthBar.addChild(outerBar);

//Add an `outer` property to the `healthBar` that references
//the `outerBar`
healthBar.outer = outerBar;
```

You can see in the last line of the preceding code that a property called `outer` has been added to `healthBar`. It just references `healthBar` (the red rectangle), so that it will be convenient to access later. You don't have to do this, but, hey, why not! It means that if you want to control the width of the red `healthBar`, you can write some smooth code that looks like this:

```
healthBar.outer.width = 30;
```

That's pretty neat and readable, so we'll keep it!

Making the Message Text

When the game is finished, some text displays "You won!" or "You lost!", depending on the outcome of the game. This is made using a text sprite and adding it to gameOverScene. Because gameOverScene's `visible` property is set to `false` when the game starts, you can't see this text. Here's the code from the setup function that creates the message text and adds it to gameOverScene:

```
message = new Text(
  "The End!",
  {font: "48px Futura"}
);
message.x = 120;
message.y = stage.height / 2 - 32;
gameOverScene.addChild(message);
```

Playing the Game

All the game logic and the code that makes the sprites move occurs inside the play function, which runs in a continuous loop. Here's an overview of what the play function does:

```
function play() {

  //Move the explorer and contain it inside the dungeon
  //Move the blob monsters
  //Check for a collision between the blobs and the explorer
  //Check for a collision between the explorer and the treasure
  //Check for a collision between the treasure and the door
  //Decide whether the game has been won or lost
  //Change the game `state` to `end` when the game is finished
}
```

Let's find out how all these features work.

Moving the Explorer

The explorer is controlled using the keyboard, and the code that does that is very similar to the keyboard control code you learned in Chapter 2. The keyboard objects modify the explorer's velocity, and that velocity is added to the explorer's position inside the play function.

```
explorer.x += explorer.vx;
explorer.y += explorer.vy;
```

The contain function we wrote in Chapter 2 is also used to keep the explorer inside the inner-wall area of dungeon.

```
contain(explorer, {x: 28, y: 10, width: 488, height: 480});
```

Figure 4-4 shows the area that the explorer's movement is limited to.

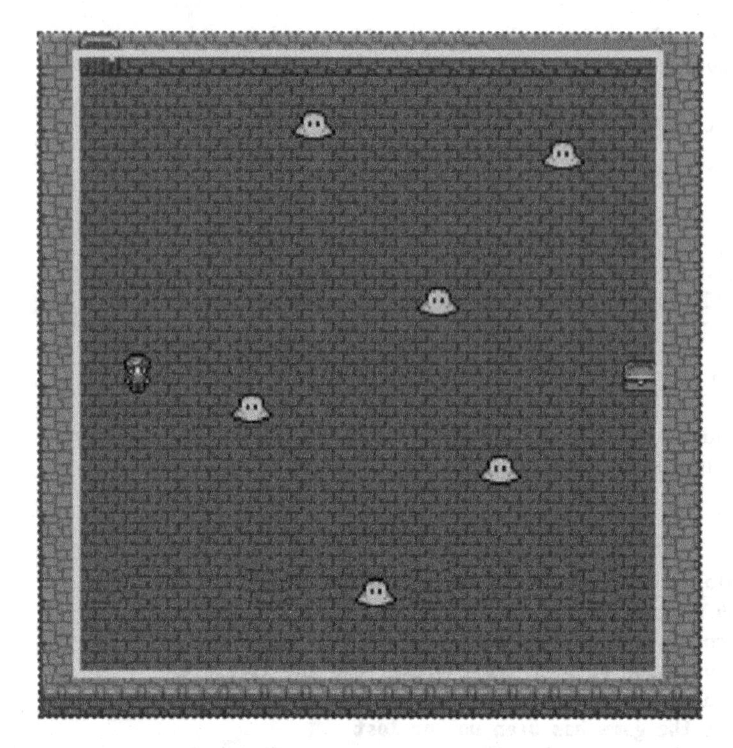

Figure 4-4. Containing the explorer's movement inside the dungeon walls

Moving the Monsters

The `play` function also moves the blob monsters, keeps them contained inside the dungeon walls, and checks each one for a collision with the player. If a blob bumps into the dungeon's top or bottom walls, its direction is reversed. All this is done with the help of a `forEach` loop, which iterates through each of the `blob` sprites in the `blobs` array on every frame.

```
blobs.forEach(blob => {

  //Move the blob
  blob.y += blob.vy;

  //Check the blob's screen boundaries
  let blobHitsWall = contain(
    blob,
    {x: 28, y: 10, width: 488, height: 480}
  );
```

```
    //If the blob hits the top or bottom of the stage, reverse its direction
    if(blobHitsWall) {
      if (blobHitsWall.has("top") || blobHitsWall.has("bottom")) {
        blob.vy *= -1;
      }
    }

    //Test for a collision. If any of the enemies are touching
    //the explorer, set `explorerHit` to `true`
    if(b.hitTestRectangle(explorer, blob)) {
      explorerHit = true;
    }
  });
```

You can see in the preceding code how the return value of the `contain` function is used to make the blobs bounce off the walls. A variable called `blobHitsWall` is used to capture the return value, as follows:

```
let blobHitsWall = contain(blob, {x: 28, y: 10, width: 488, height: 480});
```

`blobHitsWall` will usually be `undefined`. But if the blob hits the top wall, `blobHitsWall` will have the value `"top"`. If the blob hits the bottom wall, `blobHitsWall` will have the value `"bottom"`. If either of these cases is `true`, you can reverse the blob's direction by reversing its velocity. Here's the code that does this:

```
if(blobHitsWall) {
  if (blobHitsWall.has("top") || blobHitsWall.has("bottom")) {
    blob.vy *= -1;
  }
}
```

Multiplying the blob's vy (vertical velocity) value by -1 will flip the direction of its movement.

Checking for Collisions

The code in the previous section uses `hitTestRectangle` to determine if any of the enemies has touched the explorer.

```
if(b.hitTestRectangle(explorer, blob)) {
  explorerHit = true;
}
```

If `hitTestRectangle` returns `true`, it means there's been a collision, and a variable called `explorerHit` is set to `true`. If `explorerHit` is `true`, the `play` function makes the explorer semitransparent and reduces the width of the health bar by one pixel.

```
if(explorerHit) {

  //Make the explorer semi-transparent
  explorer.alpha = 0.5;

  //Reduce the width of the health bar's inner rectangle by 1 pixel
  healthBar.outer.width -= 1;

} else {

  //Make the explorer fully opaque (non-transparent) if it hasn't been hit
  explorer.alpha = 1;
}
```

If `explorerHit` is `false`, the explorer's `alpha` property is maintained at 1, which makes it fully opaque.

The `play` function also checks for a collision between the treasure chest and the explorer. If there's a hit, the `treasure` is set to the explorer's position, with a slight offset. This makes it look like the explorer is carrying the treasure, as illustrated in Figure 4-5.

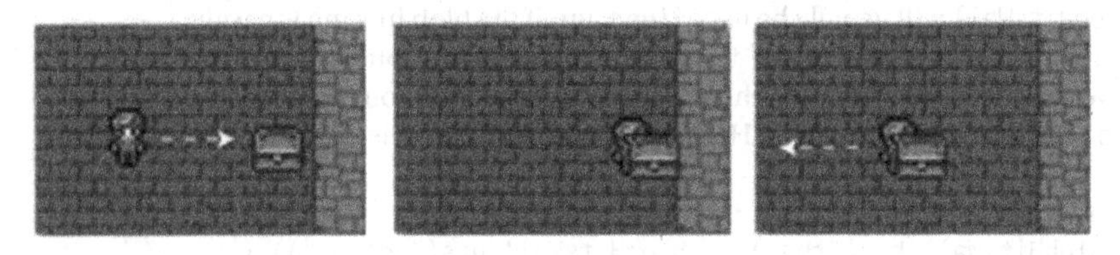

Figure 4-5. *The explorer can pick up and carry the treasure*

Here's the code that does this:

```
if (b.hitTestRectangle(explorer, treasure)) {
  treasure.x = explorer.x + 8;
  treasure.y = explorer.y + 8;
}
```

Reaching the Exit Door and Ending the Game

There are two ways the game can end. You can win if you carry the treasure to the exit, or you can lose if you run out of health.

To win the game, the treasure chest just needs to touch the exit door. If that happens, the game `state` is set to `end`, and the `message` text displays "You won."

```
if (b.hitTestRectangle(treasure, door)) {
  state = end;
  message.text = "You won!";
}
```

If you run out of health, you lose the game. The game `state` is also set to end, and the `message` text displays "You lost!"

```
if (healthBar.outer.width < 0) {
  state = end;
  message.text = "You lost!";
}
```

But what does this mean?

```
state = end;
```

You'll remember from Chapters 2 and 3 that the `gameLoop` is constantly updating a function called `state` at 60 times per second. Here's the `gameLoop` that does this:

```
function gameLoop(){
  requestAnimationFrame(gameLoop);
  state();
  renderer.render(stage);
}
```

You'll also remember that we initially set the value of `state` to `play`, which is why the `play` function runs in a loop. By setting `state` to `end`, we're telling the code that we want another function, called `end`, to run in a loop. In a more complex game, you could have a `titleScene` state, and states for each game level, such as `levelOne`, `levelTwo`, and `levelThree`.

So what is that `end` function that displays the final message? Here it is!

```
function end() {
  gameScene.visible = false;
  gameOverScene.visible = true;
}
```

It just flips the visibility of the game scenes. This is what hides `gameScene` and displays `gameOverScene` when the game ends.

This is a really simple example of how to switch a game's state, but you can have as many game states as you like in your games, and fill them with as much code as you require. Just change the value of `state` to whatever function you want to run in a loop.

■ **Note** If your game is really complex, create each game state function as a separate JavaScript file and load them with a `<script>` tag or ES6's module system. You can have as many `state` functions as you require: 10, 50, or hundreds!

And that's really all there is to Treasure Hunter! With a little more work, you could turn this simple prototype into a full game. Try it! Make sure you check out the complete code in this chapter's source files, so that you can see all the code we've looked at in its proper context.

Summary

You've seen in this chapter how you can take all the techniques you've learned in the book so far and use them to make something really exciting. The `hitTestRectangle` function is the most important collision-detection function you need to know, and it can form the basis of hundreds of different games. You also learned how to use Pixi's Containers to organize a game into different scenes, and how to switch scenes by changing the function that the `state` variable is pointing to. In addition, you learned how use game logic to determine if the game has been won or lost, and how to interactively change a sprite's property, `healthBar`, to create an interactive user interface.

Hey, you're now a game designer! And even if game design isn't your thing, you can use Treasure Hunter as a structural model for making any kind of interactive application, and scale it to any size or level of complexity. It's the only software architectural model you need to know.

Now that you've got the basics under your belt, let's find out how to make your games and applications much more engaging, by adding some interactive animation.

CHAPTER 5

Animating Sprites

So far in this book, you've learned how to make sprites, move them, and make them interactive. But what if you want to make a game character that can flap its wings, or move its arms and legs to walk around the game world? You have to use a technique called **keyframe animation**: displaying a series of slightly different images in sequence to create the illusion of motion. Pixi has some built-in tools to make keyframe animation easy, and that's what this chapter is all about.

- Using `MovieClip` sprites
- Making animation frames using a texture atlas or tileset
- Using a custom `sprite` function for full-featured control over animations
- Making a walking sprite
- Creating particle effects

The first essential step is learning how to make Pixi's `MovieClip` sprites work. So, let's find out.

Using SpriteUtilities

This chapter uses a helper library called `SpriteUtilities` that contains many helpful methods that make it much easier to create and work with Pixi sprites. You'll find `SpriteUtilities` in the `library/spriteUtilities/` folder of this book's source files, or you can find it at its online code repository: `github.com/kittykatattack/spriteUtilities`.

To use `SpriteUtilities`, link to the `spriteUtilties.js` file in your HTML document and create a new instance of it at the beginning of your program (in your `setup` function), like this:

```
let su = new SpriteUtilities(PIXI);
```

You can now access all the `SpriteUtilities` methods through this `su` object, as you'll see in the examples ahead.

MovieClip Sprites

MovieClip sprites (PIXI.extras.MovieClip) are just ordinary sprites with a few extra features that make it easy to play animated image sequences. Instead of just using one texture, a MovieClip is a sprite that uses an array of textures. Here's how you could create a new MovieClip sprite with an array of textures.

```
let textureArray = [texture0, texture1, texture2];
let sprite = new MovieClip(textureArray);
```

This loads up the sprite with three images, and you'll see ahead how you can control which image is displayed.

You can control which textures in the sequence are displayed with play, stop, gotoAndPlay, and gotoAndStop methods. You can also set the speed of the animation. MovieClip sprites are great for animated sequences or any sprites with more than one image state. Let's look at a simple example, to learn how MovieClip sprites work.

Figure 5-1 shows a PNG tileset image with a three-frame animation sequence of the pixie game character flapping her wings.

Figure 5-1. *A tileset containing animation frames*

To create an animation from those frames, you must extract each frame as a new texture and then add those textures to an array. You can then use that array of textures to make a MovieClip sprite. Here's the code that does that:

```
//Get a reference to the base texture
let base = TextureCache["images/pixieFrames.png"];

//The first texture
let texture0 = new Texture(base);
texture0.frame = new Rectangle(0, 0, 48, 32);

//The second texture
let texture1 = new Texture(base);
texture1.frame = new Rectangle(48, 0, 48, 32);

//The third texture
let texture2 = new Texture(base);
texture2.frame = new Rectangle(96, 0, 48, 32);
```

```
//Make an array of textures
let textures = [texture0, texture1, texture2];

//Create the `MovieClip` sprite using the `textures` array
let pixie = new MovieClip(textures);

//Set the sprite's position and add it to the stage
pixie.position.set(32, 32);
stage.addChild(pixie);
```

■ **Note** This bit of code just creates the `MovieClip` sprite; it doesn't make it play yet. You'll find out how to play and control `MovieClip` sprites a little further ahead.

You can see how each of the three textures was created. I coded it like this so that you can clearly see how everything fits together, but it's rather tedious to use all the repetitive code just to create three textures, so let's find a better way.

The only thing that changes for each texture is its x position on the tileset. That means you can express the x position of the three textures as an array. Each element in the array is the x position of each sequential animation frame on the tileset.

```
[0, 48, 96]
```

You can use this array to make a new array that uses those numbers to create each new texture. You could use JavaScript's array `map` method to do this. Here's how:

```
let textures = [0, 48, 96].map(x => {
  let texture = new Texture(base);
  texture.frame = new Rectangle(x, 0, 48, 32);
  return texture;
});
```

■ **Note** JavaScript's `map` method works by using the array of `x` positions to create each new texture. It then returns each created texture back to a new array called `textures`.

The Even Easier Way

Does that still seem like too much work? It does to me! So, I suggest you don't bother doing any of that and just use a helpful utility method from the `SpriteUtilities` library called `filmstrip`. Here's how to use it:

First, make sure you link the `spriteUtilities.js` file to your HTML document with a `<script>` tag, as I described at the beginning of the chapter, and then create a new instance of `SpriteUtilities`, like this:

```
let su = new SpriteUtilities(PIXI);
```

Next, use `SpriteUtilities`'s `filmstrip` method to capture all the tileset frames, like this:

```
su.filmstrip("anyTilesetImage", frameWidth, frameHeight, optionalPadding);
```

Supply `filmstrip` with the tileset image name and the width and height of each frame. If there's padding around each frame, supply the padding amount, in pixels. `filmstrip` returns an array of frames that you can use to make an animated `MovieClip` sprite. Here's how you could use `filmstrip` to create our pixie sprite from the previous example.

```
let frames = su.filmstrip("images/pixieFrames.png", 48, 32);
let pixie = new MovieClip(frames);
```

The `filmstrip` method automatically loads every frame from a tileset image into the sprite. But what if you only want to use a subset of frames from the tileset, not all of them? Use another utility method called `frames`. The `frames` method takes four arguments: the texture, a 2D array of `x`/`y` frame position coordinates, and the width and height of each frame. Here's how you could use the `frames` method to create the pixie sprite.

```
let textures = frames(
  "images/pixieFrames.png",
  [[0,0],[48,0],[96,0]],
  48, 32
);
let pixie = new MovieClip(frames);
```

Use the `frames` function whenever you have to create a sprite using selected frames from a larger tileset PNG image.

Using MovieClip Sprites

Now that you have a `MovieClip` sprite, you can make its frames play in a loop, by using the `play` method, as follows:

```
pixie.play();
```

This will make the pixie sprite flap her wings in a continuous loop. If you don't want the animation to loop, set the sprite's `loop` property to `false`.

```
pixie.loop = false;
```

Optionally, you might want to set `animationSpeed` to a slower rate, so that the pixie doesn't flap her wings too quickly.

```
pixie.animationSpeed = 0.5;
```

Use any number between 0 and 1 (1 is full speed). If your game is running at 60 frames per second, 0.5 will make the animation run at 30 frames per second.

If you want to sprite to display a specific frame, you can use the `gotoAndStop` method

```
pixie.gotoAndStop(frameNumber);
```

`gotoAndStop` will make the sprite display whichever frame number you specify. Even if your sprite isn't an animated sequence of frames, you can use `gotoAndStop` to selectively display different textures, if something good or bad happens to the sprite in a game.

■ **Note** Remember: The root stage container has to be rendered inside a game loop in order for the animation to work.

MovieClip Properties and Methods

`MovieClip` sprites have some extra properties and methods that give you a lot of control over how the animation runs, which frames to display, and what the current state of the animation is. Table 5-1 describes all the properties, and Table 5-2 describes the methods.

Table 5-1. *Properties of `MovieClip`*

MovieClip Property	Value	What It Does
`animationSpeed`	0 to 1	Changes the speed of the animation. 1 is full speed; 0 will stop the animation; 0.5 will play it at half speed
`currentFrame`	A read-only array index number	Tells you the current frame number that the `MovieClip` is displaying
`loop`	Boolean	Determines whether or not to loop the animation
`onComplete`	A function	Lets you assign a callback function that should run when the animation has finished
`playing`	Boolean	Determines whether or not `MovieClip` is currently playing
`textures`	Array	`MovieClip`'s array of textures
`totalFrames`	A read-only number	The total number of frames in the animation

Table 5-2. Methods of `MovieClip`

MovieClip Methods	Arguments	What It Does
`play`	`()` None	Starts the animation playing
`stop`	`()` None	Stops the animation
`gotoAndPlay`	`(arrayIndexNumber)`	Goes to a specific frame number and starts playing from there
`gotoAndStop`	`(arrayIndexNumber)`	Goes to a specific frame number and stops the animation
`fromImages`	`(arrayOfStrings)`	Makes a `MovieClip` from an array of image file source paths. The image will be loaded into the texture cache if it isn't already there.
`fromFrames`	`(arrayOfStrings)`	Makes a `MovieClip` from an array for texture atlas frame ids

These are the basic tools you need to know to work with Pixi's `MovieClip` sprites.

Make MovieClip Sprites Using a Texture Atlas

It's undoubtedly helpful to be able to make an animation from a few frames in any tileset PNG image, as we did in the previous example. But for a big project, you'll probably want the extra control and convenience of using a texture atlas. Let's find out how you can make a texture atlas of animation frames and then use the atlas to make a `MovieClip` sprite.

First, drag your individual frame images into Texture Packer, as shown in Figure 5-2. The game character's image files are named in a specific order, as follows:

```
pixie0.png
pixie1.png
pixie2.png
```

Figure 5-2. *Creating `MovieClip` frames using a texture atlas*

The numbers in the file names are important! They indicate the order of each frame in the animation sequence. We're going to use those numbers ahead to create the animated sprite and display the frames in the correct order.

Publish the texture atlas and load it into your Pixi program, as you learned to do in Chapter 1. In the `setup` function by which you create your sprites, use `MovieClip` to create the sprite. Supply an array of the frame ids from the texture atlas that you want to use in the animation.

```
//Create an alias for the texture atlas frame ids
id = resources["images/pixieAtlas.json"].textures;

//Create an array that references the frames you want to use
let frames = [
  id["pixie0.png"],
  id["pixie1.png"],
  id["pixie2.png"]
];

//Create a MovieClip from the frames
pixie = new MovieClip(frames);
```

You now have a sprite with three frames that you can control just as in the previous example.

Using the frameSeries Utility Function

But wait! What if you have 100 animation frames? You definitely don't want to manually type in 100 frame ids into an array. Instead, use a useful utility method from the SpriteUtilities library called frameSeries. The frameSeries function takes four arguments: the start frame sequence number, the end frame sequence number, the optional base file name, and the optional file extension. You could use the frameSeries function to create our pixie sprite from the texture atlas, like this:

```
let frames = su.frameSeries(0, 2, "pixie", ".png");
let pixie = new MovieClip(frames);
```

This automatically copies all three frames in the sequence, from 0 to 2, into the sprite.

These are the basic techniques you need to know to start using MovieClip sprites for a wide range of animation and state-change effects in games and interactive applications. But what if you want to make something much more complex, such as an animated game character that can walk around the screen?

Animation States

If you have a complex game character or interactive object, you might want that character to behave in different ways, depending on what's happening in the game environment. Each separate behavior is called a **state**. If you define states on your sprite, you can trigger those states to display whenever something significant happens in the game that corresponds to that state. In this section, you're going to learn how to define sprite states and how to control them in a game. But first, you need a few new tools to make this job a little easier.

Making a Sprite with a State Player

To start working with sprite states, you first need a **state player**. A state player is the thing that controls the sprite's states. Pixi sprites don't have their own state players, but you can use a method from the SpriteUtilities library called sprite that will create a sprite with a state player built into it.

Here's how to make a sprite using the sprite function:

```
let anySprite = su.sprite(frameTextures, xPosition, yPosition);
```

The first argument, frameTextures, can be any of the following:

- A single PNG image string
- A Pixi Texture object
- An array of texture atlas frame ids
- An array of single PNG image strings
- An array of Pixi Texture objects

You can essentially throw anything at it, and it will give you back a sprite that works as it should, depending on the kind of texture information you've supplied. That means you can use the `sprite` function as your one-stop shop for creating any kind of sprite. Forget about using Pixi's `Sprite` and `MovieClip` classes to make sprites, and just use the `sprite` method for everything!

If you supply the `sprite` method with an array, it will return a `MovieClip` sprite, but with a bonus state player built into it. The state player is just a collection of four new properties and methods that make it easy to control sprite animation states.

- **`fps`**: A property to set the precise animation speed, as frames per second. Its default value is 12. The `fps` is not linked to the game loop `fps`, and that means you can have sprite animations playing at speeds that are independent of the game or application speed.
- **`playAnimation`**: A method to play the sprite's animation. You can supply it with start and end frame values, if you want to play a subset of frames. By default, the animation will play in a loop, unless you set the sprite's `loop` property value to `false`.
- **`stopAnimation`**: A method that stops the sprite's animation at the current frame
- **`show`**: A method that displays a specific frame number

These are all the tools you require to control sprite states, so let's find out how to use them.

Defining Sprite States

What are sprite states? Take a look at Figure 5-3. It's a tileset PNG image of a game character that includes all the frames required to make the character look as if she's walking in four different directions.

Figure 5-3. *A tileset containing character animation frames*

How many sprite states are in that tileset? There are actually eight of them: four static states and four animation states. Let's find out what those states are and how to define them.

The Static States

The sprite's **static states** define four positions on the sprite when it's *not moving*. Those states are: `down`, `left`, `right`, and `up`. Figure 5-4 shows where those states are on the tileset and the frame numbers that identify those states.

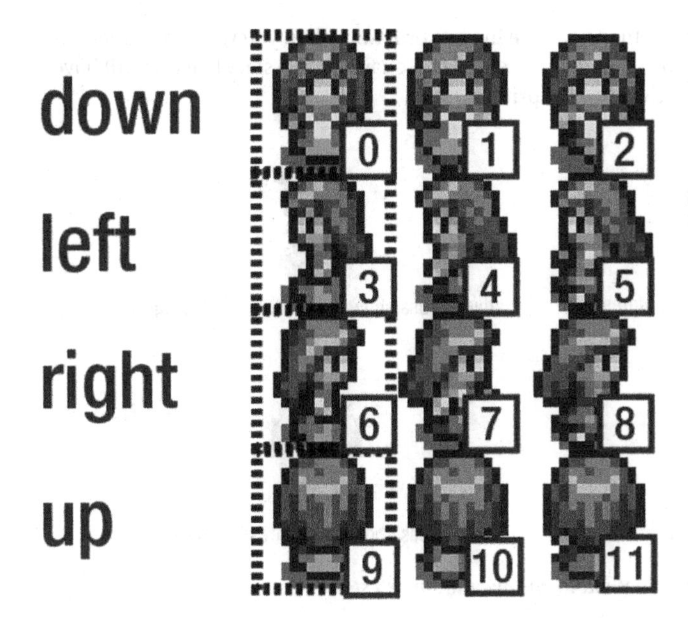

Figure 5-4. *The sprite's four static states*

You can see that frame 0 is the down state, frame 3 is the left state, frame 6 is the right state, and frame 9 is the up state. How can you define these states? First, create the sprite. This tileset image is called "adventuress.png," and here's how you could use it to create a sprite using the `sprite` method:

```
let frames = su.filmstrip("images/adventuress.png", 32, 32);
let adventuress = su.sprite(frames);
```

Next, create an object literal property on the sprite called `states`. Create keys in the object called `down`, `left`, `right`, and `up`. Set each of those keys to values that match the frame numbers of the state.

```
adventuress.states = {
  down: 0,
  left: 3,
  right: 6,
  up: 9
};
```

Now, all you have to do is use the sprite's `show` method to display the correct state. For example, here's how you could display the adventuress's `left` state:

```
adventuress.show(adventuress.states.left);
```

Use some code such as this anywhere in your program when you want to change the sprite's display state. Figure 5-5 shows the effect that changing the state like this will have on the appearance of the adventuress sprite.

adventuress.show(adventuress.states.up);

adventuress.show(adventuress.states.right);

adventuress.show(adventuress.states.left);

adventuress.show(adventuress.states.down);

Figure 5-5. *Using the* `show` *method to change the sprite's state*

Where could you use this code? Use it anywhere you need to have a sprite react to a change in the game world. An obvious place to put it would be the keyboard key press methods, so that you could change the direction the sprite is facing to match the direction of the arrow keys. For example, here's how you could make the adventuress turn to the left when the left arrow key is pressed.

```
left.press = () => {

  //Show the left state
  adventuress.show(adventuress.states.left);
};
```

Just follow this same format for the rest of the arrow keys, to make the sprite face all four directions.

Now that you know how to define and display static states, let's find out how to use animation states.

The Animation States

The sprite's **animation states** define four motion sequences of the sprite when it's *moving*. Those states are: `walkDown`, `walkLeft`, `walkRight`, and `walkUp`. Figure 5-6 shows where those states are on the tileset.

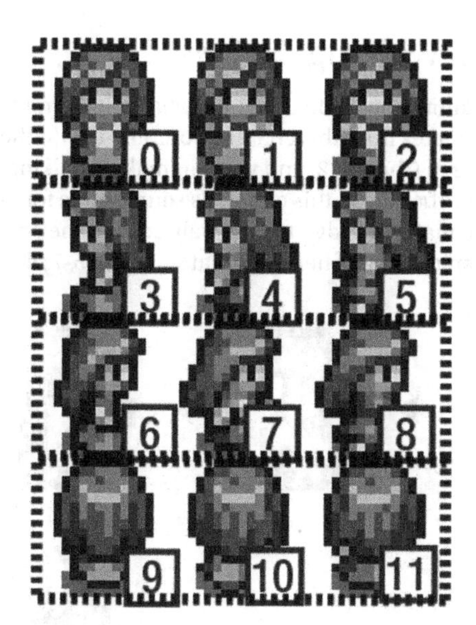

***Figure 5-6.** The sprite's four animation states*

Each of those states is comprised of three frames, which, when played in a loop, will create a continuous walking animation. To define each of these animation states, create a key in the `states` object that describes that state. The value of the key should be an array with two elements: the start frame and end frame of the sequence. For example, here's how you could define the `walkLeft` state:

```
walkLeft: [3, 5]
```

3 is the number of the frame that the animation sequence starts at, and 5 is the frame where it ends.

Here's how you could add these four new animation states to the adventuress sprite:

```
adventuress.states = {
  down: 0,
  left: 3,
  right: 6,
  up: 9,
  walkDown: [0, 2],
  walkLeft: [3, 5],
  walkRight: [6, 8],
  walkUp: [9, 11]
};
```

Now that her states are defined, let's make the adventuress walk around the stage.

Making a Walking Sprite

You already know how to do this! Take what you learned about making animated sprites and defining states from this chapter, combine it with the keyboard control code you learned to use in Chapter 2, and you can make a walking game character. Run the `statePlayer.html` file in this chapter's source code for an interactive example. Use the arrow keys to make the adventuress walk around the stage. When you release a key, she stops and displays one of her static states. Figure 5-7 illustrates the effect.

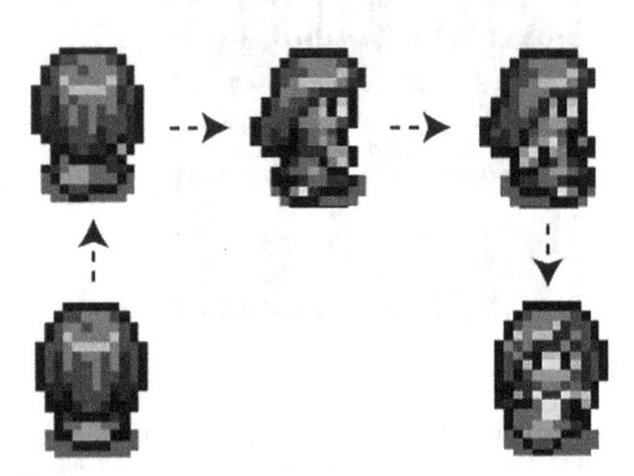

Figure 5-7. *Using the keyboard keys to make the adventuress walk*

Here's the complete code from the program's `setup` function that creates the sprite and programs the keyboard keys:

```
//Define any variables that are used in more than one function
let adventuress;

function setup() {

  //Use the custom `frameSeries` function to create the frames array
  let frames = filmstrip("images/adventuress.png", 32, 32);

  //Create a MovieClip from the frames using the
  //custom `sprite` utility function
  adventuress = sprite(frames);
  adventuress.vx = 0;
  adventuress.vy = 0;

  //Set the sprite's position and add it to the stage
  adventuress.position.set(32, 32);
  stage.addChild(adventuress);
```

```
//Optionally set the sprite's `fps` to change the
//speed of the animation effect (the default value is 12)
adventuress.fps = 12

//Define the sprite's states
adventuress.states = {
  down: 0,
  left: 3,
  right: 6,
  up: 9,
  walkDown: [0, 2],
  walkLeft: [3, 5],
  walkRight: [6, 8],
  walkUp: [9, 11]
};

//Capture the keyboard arrow keys
let left = keyboard(37),
    up = keyboard(38),
    right = keyboard(39),
    down = keyboard(40);

//Program the arrow keys

//Left arrow key `press` method
left.press = () => {

  //Play the sprite's `walkLeft` animation
  //sequence and set the sprite's velocity
  adventuress.playAnimation(adventuress.states.walkLeft);
  adventuress.vx = -5;
  adventuress.vy = 0;
};

//Left arrow key `release` method
left.release = () => {

  //If the left arrow has been released, and the right arrow isn't down,
  //and the sprite isn't moving vertically, stop the sprite from moving
  //by setting its velocity to zero. Then display the sprite's static
  //`left` state.
  if (!right.isDown && adventuress.vy === 0) {
    adventuress.vx = 0;
    adventuress.show(adventuress.states.left);
  }
};
```

```
  //The rest of the arrow keys follow the same format

  //Up
  up.press = () => {
    adventuress.playAnimation(adventuress.states.walkUp);
    adventuress.vy = -5;
    adventuress.vx = 0;
  };
  up.release = () => {
    if (!down.isDown && adventuress.vx === 0) {
      adventuress.vy = 0;
      adventuress.show(adventuress.states.up);
    }
  };

  //Right
  right.press = () => {
    adventuress.playAnimation(adventuress.states.walkRight);
    adventuress.vx = 5;
    adventuress.vy = 0;
  };
  right.release = () => {
    if (!left.isDown && adventuress.vy === 0) {
      adventuress.vx = 0;
      adventuress.show(adventuress.states.right);
    }
  };

  //Down
  down.press = () => {
    adventuress.playAnimation(adventuress.states.walkDown);
    adventuress.vy = 5;
    adventuress.vx = 0;
  };
  down.release = () => {
    if (!up.isDown && adventuress.vx === 0) {
      adventuress.vy = 0;
      adventuress.show(adventuress.states.down);
    }
  };

  //Start the game loop
  gameLoop();
}
```

The play function (which gets called each frame by the game loop) is what makes the sprite move around the screen.

```
function play() {
  adventuress.x += adventuress.vx;
  adventuress.y += adventuress.vy;
}
```

If you want the sprite to move faster or slower across the screen, change, in the arrow key methods, the amount by which vx and vy are set. If you want the sprite's walking animation effect to be faster or slower, change the sprite's fps property.

Yes, you can use this in a real game! Take a look at the treasureHunter2.html file in this chapter's source files, for a new, updated version of Treasure Hunter, featuring our fully animated adventuress sprite, shown in Figure 5-8. Use the arrow keys to make her walk around the dungeon. The code is exactly the same as the original version, but with the addition of the new code you've learned in this chapter.

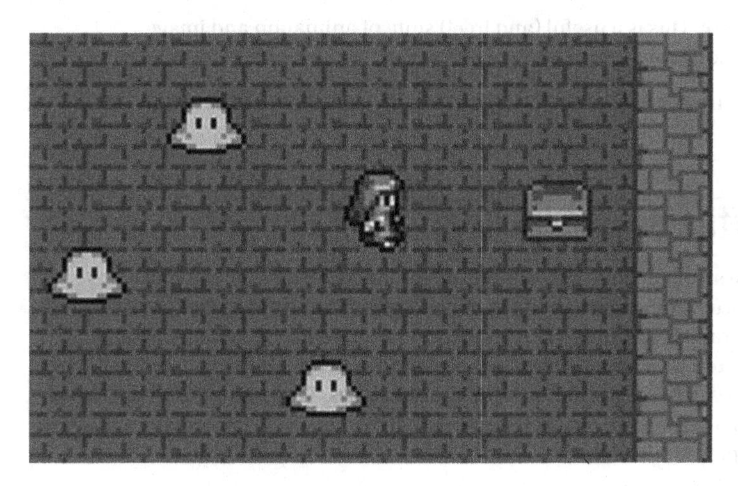

Figure 5-8. *A walking sprite in Treasure Hunter*

Adding keyframe animation to the sprite makes the game feel much more immersive.

In this chapter, I've shown you how to control a sprite's animation states, using a keyboard controller, but any change in the game logic could change the sprite's state. In Chapter 7, you'll learn how to make interactive sprites, using the mouse and touch.

Creating Frames for Animations

You've learned how to program animated game characters from preexisting tilesets, but how do you actually make those animation tilesets themselves? That topic deserves a whole book on its own, but fortunately, there are some great illustration and animation tools out there to help make this job easy and fun. You could use Adobe Illustrator or

Photoshop to draw each frame by hand, or you could use specialized animation software, such as any of the following:

- **Flash Professional**. Still the best all-purpose animation tool out there. Just export your animation as a spritesheet, and you can use it in your JavaScript games. You can also use a tool such as Shoebox to convert Flash's SWF file format to a texture atlas.
- **Piskel**. A fun, free online tool for making pixel art-style animated game characters.
- **Dragon Bones**, **Spine**, and **Creature**. These three tools are all very similar. They let you create complex game characters, animate them, and export them as tileset images and JSON files. Try them out and see which you prefer. Pixi v3.0 actually has limited import capability for Dragon Bones and Spine animation. Check Pixi's current documentation for details.
- **Shoebox**. This is a useful (and free!) suite of animation and image extraction tools.

Spend an afternoon playing around with some of these tools and see what you can create.

Particle Effects

How do you create such effects as fire, smoke, magic, and explosions? You make lots of tiny sprites—dozens, hundreds, or thousands of them. Then apply some physical or gravitational constraints to those sprites, so that they behave like the element you're trying to simulate. You also have to give them some rules about how they should appear and disappear and what kinds of patterns they should form. These tiny sprites are called **particles**. You can use them to make a wide range of special effects for games. In this last section of the chapter, you're going to learn how to create animated particles.

Add a Little Pixi Dust

Pixi doesn't have a built-in feature for making particle effects, but you can use a lightweight micro-library called Dust to help you make them. To use Dust, link to the `dust.js` application file in this book's source code library or download it from its code repository: `github.com/kittykatattack/dust`.

■ **Note** Dust is a quick and easy way to make most of the kinds of particle effects you'll need for games, but for a more full-featured, but also more complex, library, take a look at Proton: `github.com/a-jie/Proton`.

To get started with Dust, first create an instance of it at the beginning of your program, or in the `setup` function, and supply `PIXI` in the constructor, as follows:

```
d = new Dust(PIXI);
```

The variable `d` now represents your running instance of Dust.

Next, it is very important to make sure that you call Dust's `update` function inside your game loop. In the application model that we've been using in this book, you could do this inside either the `gameLoop` or `play` function. I recommend that you do it in `gameLoop`, just after you call the `state` function but before you render the stage, like this:

```
function gameLoop(){
  requestAnimationFrame(gameLoop);
  state();
  d.update();
  renderer.render(stage);
}
```

You're now ready to use Dust to make and animate particles.

Making Particles

With Dust all set up and running, you can now make particles using the `create` method. Here's how to create 50 star sprites on the stage at an x/y position of 128/128.

```
let stars = d.create(
  128,                                 //x start position
  128,                                 //y start position
  () => su.sprite("images/star.png"),  //Sprite function
  stage,                               //Container for particles
  50                                   //Number of particles
);
```

The first two arguments are the x/y point on which the particles will appear. The third argument is a function that returns the sprite you want to use for each particle. Use any sprite creation method we've used in this book. If you supply a sprite with more than one frame, Dust will randomly display different frames for each particle. The fourth argument is the container that you want to add the particles to. In this example, the particles will be added to the stage. The fifth argument is the number of particles you want to create. The `create` method returns an array containing references to all the sprites being used as particles, which might be useful if you have to access them for reasons such as performing collision detection.

Figure 5-9 shows the effect that this code produces. The particles appear at the same point with different random sizes and velocities. They fly away from the center point, randomly changing scale and alpha, until they all fade away and disappear. Many of the properties are randomized, so the effect is different every time. You'll see ahead how you can fine-tune each of these properties to produce exactly the effect you need.

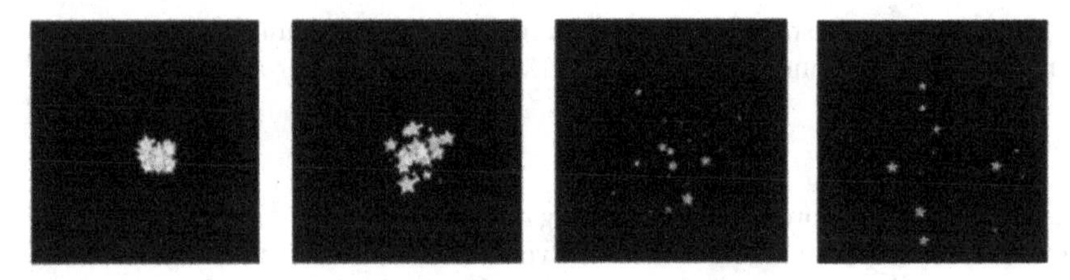

Figure 5-9. A starburst particle effect

You can drop this code anywhere in your program, to create a single burst of particles, such as a key press or mouse click. (You'll learn about mouse and touch interactivity in Chapter 7).

Using ParticleContainer

In the preceding sample code, the particles that we created were all added to the root `stage` container (the fourth argument.) However, you can add the particles to any container you like, or to any other sprite. In Chapter 2, you learned how to make a high-performance `ParticleContainer` for displaying a large number of sprites on screen at a high frame rate. If you want to use `ParticleContainer` for your particles, just add the name of the `ParticleContainer` object you want to use in the `create` method's fourth argument. Here's how you could modify the preceding sample code to add the particles to a `ParticleContainer` called `starContainer`.

```
//Create the `ParticleContainer` and add it to the `stage`
let starContainer = new ParticleContainer(
  15000,
  {alpha: true, scale: true, rotation: true, uvs: true}
);
stage.addChild(starContainer);

//Create star particles and add them to the `starContainer`
let stars = d.create(
  128, 128,
  () => su.sprite("images/star.png"),
  starContainer,
  50
);
```

`ParticleContainers` are optimized for pushing many thousands of sprites, so, unless you're animating that many particles, you probably won't notice any performance improvement over using ordinary `Container` objects.

Customizing the Particle Options

The create method has a total of 19 different parameters you can set to fully customize how the particles behave. Here's the full parameter list, with examples of the kinds of values you could use:

```
let stars = d.create(
  128,                                 //x start position
  128,                                 //y start position
  () => su.sprite("images/star.png"), //Sprite function
  stage                                //Container for particles
  50,                                  //Number of particles
  0.1,                                 //Gravity
  true,                                //Random spacing
  0, 6.28,                             //Min/max angle
  12, 24,                              //Min/max size
  1, 2,                                //Min/max speed
  0.005, 0.01,                         //Min/max scale speed
  0.005, 0.01,                         //Min/max alpha speed
  0.05, 0.1                            //Min/max rotation speed
);
```

You can see that most of the parameters describe a range between the minimum and maximum values that should be used to change the sprites' speed, rotation, scale, or alpha. You can also specify the number of particles that should be created and add optional gravity.

The minimum and maximum angle values are important for defining the circular spread of particles as they radiate from the origin point. For a completely circular explosion effect, use a minimum angle of 0 and a maximum angle of 6.28.

```
0, 6.28
```

(These values are radians; the equivalents in degrees are 0 and 360.) 0 starts at the 3 o'clock position, pointing directly to the right. 3.14 is the 9 o'clock position, and 6.28 takes you around back to 0 again.

If you want to constrain the particle range to a narrower angle, just supply the minimum and maximum values that describe that angle. Here are values you could use to constrain the angle to a pizza-slice with the crust pointing left:

```
2.4, 3.6
```

You could use a constrained angle range such as this to create a particle stream, like those used to create a fountain or rocket engine flames. (You'll see exactly how to do this in the example ahead.) The random spacing value (the seventh argument) determines whether the particles should be spaced evenly (false) or randomly (true) within this range.

By carefully choosing the sprite for the particle and finely adjusting each parameter, you can use this all-purpose create function to simulate everything from liquid to fire.

Using a Particle Emitter

The `create` method produces a single burst of particles, but often you'll have to produce a continuous stream of particles. You can do this with the help of a **particle emitter**. A particle emitter produces particles at fixed intervals to produce just such a stream effect, and you can create one using Dust's `emitter` method. The emitter has `play` and `stop` methods that let you turn the particle flow on and off, and you can define the interval at which particles are created.

Here's the general format for using Dust's `emitter` method. It takes two arguments. The first argument is the interval, in milliseconds, between which bursts of particles are created. The second argument is the same `create` method we used in the previous examples.

```
let particleStream = d.emitter(
  100,
  () => d.create();
);
```

Any interval value of 100 milliseconds or less will make the particles appear to flow in a continuous stream. Here's some code that produces a star fountain effect, illustrated in Figure 5-10. The stars appear in the center of the canvas, shoot up, and then cascade down with the pull of gravity.

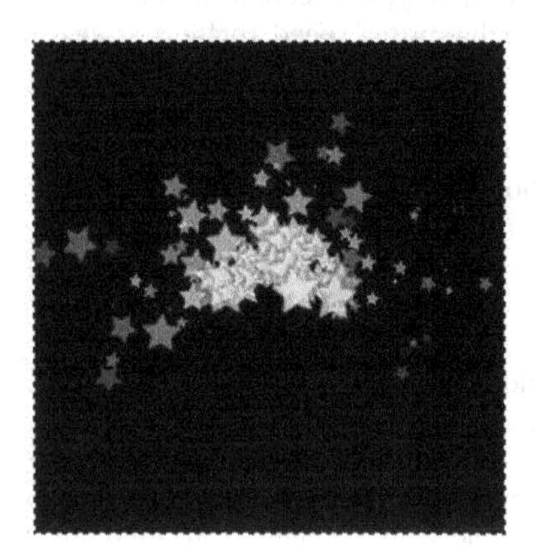

Figure 5-10. *Using a particle emitter to produce a continuous stream of particles*

```
let particleStream = d.emitter(
  100,
  () => d.create(
    128, 128,
    () => su.sprite("images/star.png"),
    stars,
    30,
    0.1,
```

```
    false,
    3.14, 6.28,
    16, 32,
    2, 5
  )
);
```

The sixth argument, 0.1, is the force of gravity. Setting gravity to a higher number will pull the particles down faster. (Set gravity to 0 to turn it off.) The angle is between 3.14 and 6.28. That makes the particles appear within a half-moon sized angle above their origin point. Figure 5-11 illustrates how that angle is defined.

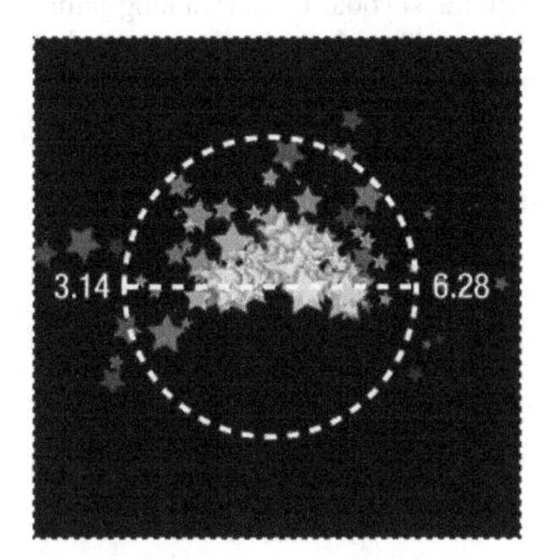

Figure 5-11. *Limiting the angle within which particles are created*

The stars are created at the center origin point then fly up and out within the upper half of the circle. Gravity is acting on the particles the entire time, however, so they'll eventually fall toward the bottom of the canvas. That's what creates the cascading fountain effect.

You can use the emitter's `play` and `stop` methods to turn the particle stream on or off at any time in your code, like this:

```
particleStream.play();
particleStream.stop();
```

This is all you need to know to start working with particle effects for Pixi.

Summary

In this chapter, you've learned all the important skills you need for making interactive game characters and objects. You learned how to load up `MovieClip` sprites with frames and how to use those frames to display different object states. This alone is one of the most important techniques to know, because it lets you change the visual appearance of a sprite to react to changes in the game or application. And, as a bonus, you learned how to use the custom `sprite` utility function to make this job easy and intuitive. You also learned how to make sprites from almost any kind of source: single tileset PNG images, texture atlas frame id sequences, and even subsets of frames inside a larger tileset. You put all these techniques together to make a very complex object—a walking game character—that you could control and move with the keyboard. That walking game character is the key to making much more complex interactive objects, if you ever need to. And finally, you learned how to use the Dust library to easily create all kinds of particle effects for games.

Particle effects are a great way to add sparkle to any game, but in the next chapter, you're going to learn a boatload of cool visual effects that you can easily implement with Pixi. Let's find out!

CHAPTER 6

Visual Effects and Transitions

Pixi is a high-powered 2D rendering engine packed with all kinds of useful tools to help you make spectacular visual effects with minimal effort. In this chapter, you're going to learn all the techniques and code you need to know to get those tools working for you quickly, including the following:

- **Tiling sprites**. A quick way to scroll a seamlessly repeating pattern
- **Texture effects**. Specialized methods for working with textures
- **Tinting**. Changes a sprite's color
- **Masking**. A shape that hides any part of the sprite that's outside of the shape's area.
- **Blend modes**. Determine how semitransparent sprites blend together
- **Filters**. A wide range of built-in distortion, blur and color effects
- **Video textures**. Play a video on a sprite
- **Multiple resolutions**. Automatically load different images to match the device display resolution
- **Rope mesh**. Move a series of points along a texture to create a wave effect
- **Tweening and transitions**. A handful of useful methods for quickly animating sprite properties.

This chapter is a fast-paced grand tour of all these techniques, which, as you'll soon see, you'll easily be able to implement into your own work.

Tiling Sprites

The first stop on the tour: **tiling sprites**. These are special sprites that repeat an image across their surface in a grid pattern. You can use them to easily create infinitely scrolling background effects. To create a tiling sprite, use the `TilingSprite` class (`PIXI.extras.TilingSprite`) with three arguments: texture, width, and height.

```
let tilingSprite = new TilingSprite(texture, width, height);
```

Apart from that, tiling sprites have all the same properties and work in the same way as regular sprites. They also have `fromImage` and `fromFrame` methods, like ordinary sprites. Here's how to create a tiling sprite from a single 64 by 65 image called tile.png. It's 192 by 192 pixels and is offset from the top of the canvas by 32 pixels.

```
let tilingSprite =  new TilingSprite(
  TextureCache["images/tile.png"], 192, 192
);
sprite.x = 32;
sprite.y = 32;
```

Figure 6-1 shows the original tile.png image and the effect of the preceding code.

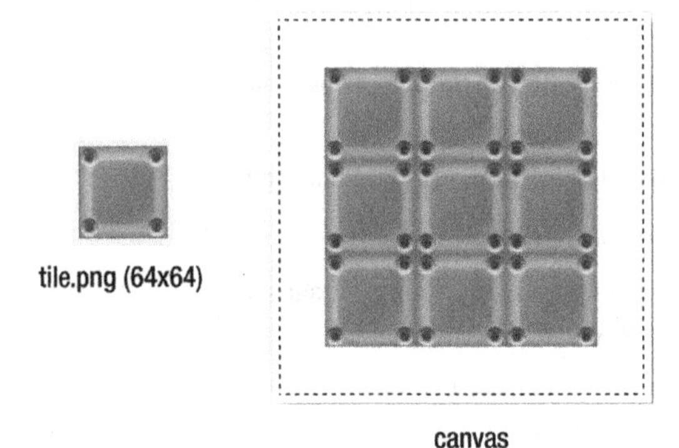

Figure 6-1. *Creating a sprite with a repeating image pattern*

You can offset the repeating pattern using `tilePosition.x` and `tilePosition.y` properties. Here's how to offset the pattern by 32 pixels.

```
sprite.tilePosition.x = 32;
sprite.tilePosition.y = 32;
```

Figure 6-2 shows the result.

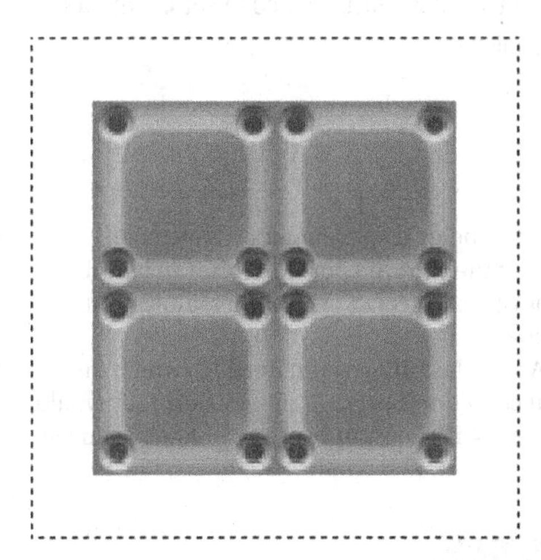

Figure 6-2. *Using `tilePosition` to offset the pattern*

You can also change the scale of the repeated image using `tileScale.x` and `tileScale.y`. Here's how to increase the size of the repeated image by one and a half times:

```
sprite.tileScale.x = 1.5;
sprite.tileScale.y = 1.5;
```

Figure 6-3 shows what this does.

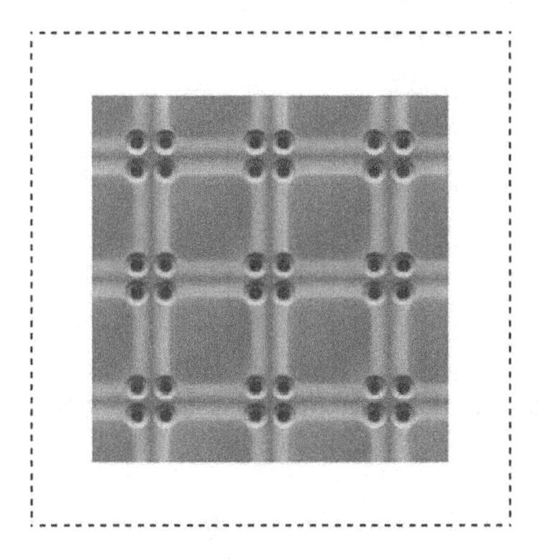

Figure 6-3. *Using `tileScale` to change the size of the image in the pattern*

■ **Note** As with the `position` property, you can use the `set` method to set `tileScale` and `tilePosition` with one line of code, as follows:

```
sprite.tilePosition.set(32, 32);
sprite.tileScale.set(1.5, 1.5);
```

There's much more to tiling sprites than just being a convenient way to create repeating image patterns. Because you can shift the texture's position, you can use tiling sprites to easily create seamless, scrolling background scenes. This is incredibly useful for many kinds of games. Let's find out how to do this.

First, start with a **seamless tile image**. A seamless image is an image in which the patterns match up on all sides. If you laid out copies of the image side by side, they would appear to be one big continuous image. Figure 6-4 is an example of a seamless tile image of a cloudy sky.

Figure 6-4. *A seamless tile image*

Next, create a tiling sprite called `clouds`, using this image. Then update the sprite's `tilePosition.x` property in the game loop.

```
function play() {
  clouds.tilePosition.x -= 1;
}
```

When you run this code, the clouds appear to scroll infinitely, from the left, across the canvas, as illustrated in Figure 6-5.

***Figure 6-5.** Using a tiling sprite to easily create an infinitely scrolling background effect*

You can use this feature to create an impressive pseudo 3D effect called **parallax scrolling**. Here's how: layer multiple tiling sprites like this at the same position, and make the images that are supposed to be farther away move slower than the ones that are supposed to be closer. Try it!

Tools for Working with Textures

Pixi has three useful tools for working with sprite textures: `generateTexture`, `cacheAsBitmap`, and the `RenderTexture` class.

Using generateTexture

Pixi lets you generate a texture from a `Graphics` or `Sprite` object, using the `generateTexture` method. Here's how to use it:

```
let triangleTexture = triangle.generateTexture();
```

You can then use that texture to create a new sprite.

```
let triangleSprite = new Sprite(triangleTexture);
```

This is great for creating new sprites from existing sprites dynamically while your game is running.

Using cacheAsBitmap

A related property is cacheAsBitmap. Imagine that you have a Container or Sprite object that contains thousands of child sprites. Instead of making Pixi process and render each and every child, cacheAsBitmap will display the whole container as one single image. To use cacheAsBitmap, just set it to true on any Sprite or DisplayObjectContainer object.

```
sprite.cacheAsBitmap = true;
```

If any child sprites inside the container are moving, they'll freeze in place. Set cacheAsBitmap back to false to make the parent render as usual and un-freeze the child sprites. cacheAsBitmap is a great optimization whenever you need to flatten lots objects or complex nested sprites into one single object.

Using RenderTexture

The third little trick you need to know is how to use a RenderTexture (PIXI.RenderTexture) object. RenderTexture is a special kind of texture that lets you project a sprite onto another sprite. It allows for all kinds of quirky mirror-like effects. Here's how to create RenderTexture and use it to make a new sprite (only the first argument is required):

```
renderTexture = new RenderTexture(
  renderer, width, height, scaleMode, resolution
);
let sprite = new Sprite(renderTexture);
```

Now use the renderTexture's render method to render any other sprite's texture onto the original sprite.

```
renderTexture.render(anyOtherSprite);
```

The original sprite's texture will now have the same texture as anyOtherSprite. If the other sprite's texture is being animated using tilePosition or tileScale, the original sprite's texture will also animate.

RenderTexture's render method has three arguments (only the first is required).

```
renderTexture.render(sprite, position, clear);
```

The second argument, position, is a Point object (PIXI.Point) object that defines the sprite's x and y position. You can use the sprite's position object for this. But you can also create a Point object directly, as follows:

```
let point = new Point(xPosition, yPosition);
```

You can then access the point's values, as follows:

```
point.x
point.y
```

The `render` method's third argument, `clear`, is a Boolean that determines whether the texture should be cleared before the sprite is drawn.

With a bit of creativity, things can get really funky, really fast. What would happen if you rendered a texture back into itself? Figure 6-6 shows a complex example from Pixi's web site.

Figure 6-6. *Using `RenderTexture` to render any sprite to a dynamic texture*

Tinting

Sprites have a `tint` property that lets you change their color. Here's how to change the tint of three sprites to yellow, red and green, respectively.

```
cat.tint = 0xFFFF660;
tiger.tint = 0x66FF66;
hedgehog.tint = 0xFF6666;
```

Figure 6-7 shows the effect this has.

Figure 6-7. *Setting a tint property to change a sprite's color*

The default tint for every sprite is white (0xFFFFFF), which essentially means, "no tint." Use tinting whenever you want to change a sprite's color without completely changing its texture.

Masking

Pixi lets you use a `Graphics` object to mask any sprite (or a container with nested child sprites). A mask is a shape that hides any part of the sprite that's outside of the shape's area. To use a mask, create a `Sprite` and a `Graphics` object. Then set the sprite's `mask` property to the shape.

```
sprite.mask = shape;
```

Figure 6-8 shows an example. First, an ordinary `cat` sprite is created. A red `square` is then created and positioned over the `cat` (the color of the shape doesn't matter, but red is traditional for masks). Last, the `cat`'s `mask` property is set to the `square`. This cuts out the image of the `cat` that's inside the area of the `square`. Any part of the `cat` that's outside that area isn't visible.

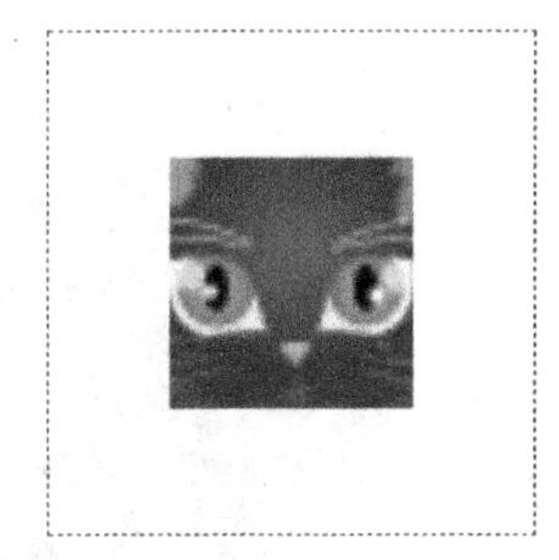

Figure 6-8. *Using a shape to mask a sprite*

Here's an abridged version of the code that creates this effect.

```
let cat = new Sprite(id["cat.png"]);
//... create the cat...

let rectangle = new Graphics();
//... create the rectangle...

//Mask the cat with the rectangle
cat.mask = rectangle;
```

You can also animate masks for interesting layering effects.

Blend Modes

The `blendMode` property determines how semitransparent sprites blend with images below them. You have a choice of 17, which are listed ahead. Apply them to a sprite, like this:

```
sprite.blendMode = PIXI.BLEND_MODES.MULTIPLY;
```

Figure 6-9 shows three semitransparent sprites with their blend modes set to `MULTIPLY`.

Figure 6-9. *Using blend modes to enhance transparency effects*

Here's a full list of the blend modes you can use, and the effect each produces:

- **NORMAL**. No blending
- **SOFT_LIGHT**, **HARD_LIGHT**, **OVERLAY**. Contrast
- **LIGHTEN**, **COLOR_DODGE**, **SCREEN**. Lightening
- **DARKEN**, **COLOR_BURN**, **MULTIPLY**. Darkening
- **DIFFERENCE**, **EXCLUSION**. Color inversion
- **HUE**, **SATURATION**, **COLOR**, **LUMINOSITY**, **ADD**. Complex blending

These are the same transparency blend modes used in image editors (such as Photoshop, Pixelmator, or Gimp). The best way to appreciate the subtle effect of each blend mode is to open some images in an image editor, apply these blend modes to them, and observe the effect. If you're feeling overwhelmed by choice, I suggest you just use `MULTIPY` for a darkening effect or `SCREEN` for a lightening effect.

Filters

Pixi has a wide range of filters that let you apply distortion effects to sprites in real time. (All the filters are in the `PIXI.filters` object.) Filters are one of Pixi's best features, because they let you easily create dramatic effects that would otherwise only be possible with complex, low-level WebGL programming.

Here's an example of how to create a BlurFilter (the other filters follow the same format):

```
//Create the filter
let blurFilter = new PIXI.filters.BlurFilter();

//Set any of the filter's properties
blurFilter.blur = 20;

//Add the filter to the sprite's `filters` array
cat.filters = [blurFilter];
```

All Pixi DisplayObjects (Sprite and Container objects) have a filters array. To add a filter to a sprite, create the filter and just add it to the sprite's filters array. You can add as many filters as you like.

```
cat.filters = [blurFilter, sepiaFilter, displacementFilter];
```

Manage it just like you would any other ordinary array. To clear all of a sprite's filters, just clear the array.

```
cat.filters = [];
```

Table 6-1 is a list of Pixi's currently supported filters, and the properties you can set on them.

Table 6-1. *Pixi's supported filters and their properties*

Filter	Properties	What It Does
AsciiFilter	size: The pixel size of the area that should be converted into characters	Displays the image using ASCII text characters
AlphaMaskFilter	map: A texture	Uses alpha pixel values from the map texture to let you create mask effects with gradients
BloomFilter	blur: The amount of blur, in pixels, on both the x and y axis blurX: The amount of x axis blur blurY: The amount of y axis blur (The default for these is 2.)	A natural-looking Gaussian blur, which is great for diffuse lighting effects

(*continued*)

Table 6-1. (*continued*)

Filter	Properties	What It Does
BlurDirFilter	dirX: The blur in the x direction dirY: The blur in the y direction	Applies a Gaussian blur in a specific direction. (There are also two separate filters, BlurXFilter and BlurYFilter, if you just want a blur in one direction.)
BlurFilter	blur: The x and y blur amount blurX: Amount of blur on the x axis blurY: Amount of blur on the y axis.	Makes the sprite blurry, in a slightly less pretty but slightly better performing way than the BloomFilter
ColorMatrixFilter	matrix: An array of 16 numbers. Each set of 4 numbers represents a color: red, green, blue, alpha.	Gives you fine control over color effects. Lets you apply a 4 by 4 matrix transformation on the RGBA color and alpha values of every pixel on DisplayObject to produce a result with a new set of RGBA color and alpha values. Lets you create luminance, alpha, and saturation effects
ColorStepFilter	step: A number by which to lower the color depth	Lets you lower the color detail of an image, for a flatter color effect
CrossHatchFilter	None	Creates a crosshatch effect and makes the sprite appear to be shaded by short, intersecting diagonal lines
DisplacementFilter	map: A texture scale: The multiplier used to scale the displacement	Warps a sprite based on pixel values in the map texture
DotScreenFilter	angle: The angle, in radians, that the dots are tilted scale: The size of the dot (0 to 1)	Makes sprites appear to be made of black dots, like comic book newsprint

(*continued*)

Table 6-1. *(continued)*

Filter	Properties	What It Does
`DropShadowFilter`	`alpha`: The transparency (0 to 1) `angle`: The shadow angle, in radians. `blur`: Simultaneously sets the x and y axis blur to the same amount (a number in pixels) `blurX`: Blur on the x axis `blurY`: Blur on the y axis `color`: The shadow color `distance`: The shadow distance, in pixels	Creates a drop-shadow
`GrayFilter`	`gray`: The amount of grayness. 0 is none (white); 1 is full (black).	Adds grayness to the sprite
`InvertFilter`	`invert`: 0 to 1. 0 won't invert the colors; 1 inverts them completely.	Inverts the sprite's colors
`PixelateFilter`	`size`: the size of the pixels. A `Point` object with x and y values that describe its width and the height of the blocks in pixels. x is the width of the block, y is the height.	Makes the sprite appear pixelated (blocky)
`SepiaFilter`	`sepia`: The strength of the sepia effect (0 to 1)	Adds a yellow-brown tint to the sprite to make it look like an old photograph
`ShockwaveFilter`	`center`: An object that contains two normalized (0 to 1) values that sets the center point of the shockwave on the sprite. For example, the value `{x: 0.5, y: 0.5}` sets it to the dead center of the sprite. `time`: The duration, in milliseconds, that the shockwave should ripple out from the center point	An animated effect that produces a color shockwave that ripples across a sprite
`TwistFilter`	`angle`: The angle of the twist, in radians `offset`: A `Point` object that describes the offset of the twist `radius`: The radius, in pixels, of the twist	Twists the sprite

(continued)

Table 6-1. *(continued)*

Filter	Properties	What It Does
RGBSplitFilter	red: A Point object that sets the red channel offset green: A Point object that sets the green channel offset blue: A Point object that sets the blue channel offset	Splits the Red, Green, Blue and Alpha channels to make the sprite looks as if it's being displayed by a misaligned video projector
SmartBlurFilter	None	Similar to the BlurFilter, but it produces a slightly different effect
TiltShiftFilter	start: The y value to start the effect end: The y value to end the effect blur: The strength of the blur. Values between 0 and 10 look good. gradientBlur: The strength of the gradient blur	Creates a **tilt-shift** effect: a blurring effect that makes images look like small, shiny plastic toys. (There's also a TiltShiftXFilter and a TiltShiftYFilter, for applying the effect on one axis only. There's also a TiltShiftAxisFilter, which is used by Pixi under the hood to help these other filters. You don't have to use it directly.)

In addition to these properties, all filters also include additional padding and uniforms properties. padding adds space around the filter area. uniforms is an object that can be used to send extra values to the WebGL renderer. In day-to-day use, you'll never have to worry about setting the uniforms property.

The best way to see the effect of these filters is an interactive demonstration on Pixi's web site (www.goodboydigital.com/pixijs/examples/15/indexAll.html), shown in Figure 6-10.

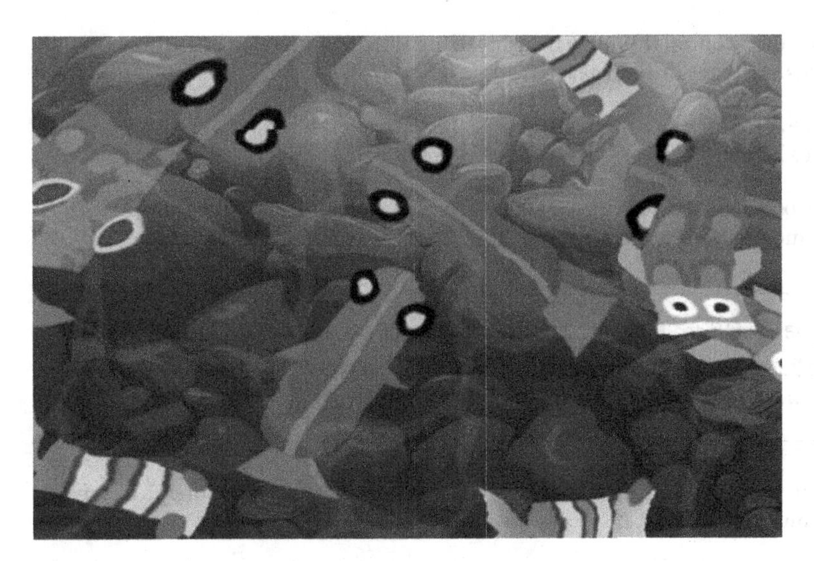

Figure 6-10. *Dynamic filter effects*

Note Pixi's filters only work with the `WebGLRenderer`, because the Canvas Drawing API is too slow to update them in real time.

Video Textures

You can use a video as a texture for a sprite just as easily as you can use an image. First, load the video using Pixi's loader, the same way you would load an image or JSON file. Then use the `Texture` class's `fromVideo` method to create a video texture.

```
let videoTexture = Texture.fromVideo("videoFile.mp4");
let videoSprite = new Sprite(videoTexture);
stage.addChild(videoSprite);
```

(Alternatively, you can use the `Texture.fromVideoUrl` method to create a video texture from a URL address.)

The video texture is just an ordinary HTML5 video element, which you can access through the texture's `baseTexture.source` property, as follows:

```
let videoSource = videoTexture.baseTexture.source;
```

You can then control the video with any of the HTML5 video element's properties and methods, such as play and pause.

```
videoSource.play();
videoSource.stop();
```

Take a look at the HTML video element's full specification, for a list of all the properties and methods you can use.

■ **Note** The fromVideo method has a second optional parameter: scaleMode. This determines the algorithm that is used to scale pixels if the size of the texture changes and can be any of the three SCALE_MODE values.

Hey, are you keeping up? Our whistle-stop tour is halfway over, but there's lots more to come. Onward!

Working with Multiple Resolutions

Pixi automatically adjusts the pixel density to match the resolution of the device that your content is running on. All you have to do is provide different images, at high resolutions and low resolutions, and Pixi will help you choose the correct one based on the current device resolution.

■ **Note** When you're creating high res images, add "@2x" to the image file name to indicate that the image is double resolution (for "retina" display, for example). This sets the resolution property on the sprite's baseTexture property (sprite.texture.baseTexture.resolution).

The first step is to find out what the current resolution is. You can do this using the window.devicePixelRatio method. Assign this value to a variable.

```
let displayResolution = window.devicePixelRatio;
```

displayResolution will be a number that describes your resolution. It's automatically provided by the device running your application. 1 is standard resolution; 2 is high-density resolution; and you'll increasingly find some super high-density displays that report 3.

The next step is to assign this value to the resolution property of the render's options. Do this when you create the renderer, as follows:

```
let renderer = autoDetectRenderer(
  800, 600, {resolution: displayResolution}
);
```

Then selectively load the correct image into a texture, based on the resolution. Here's how:

```
let texture;
if (displayResolution === 2) {

  //Load the high resolution image
  texture = TextureCache["highResImage@2x.png"];

} else {

  //Load the normal resolution image
  texture = TextureCache["normalResImage.png");
}
let anySprite = new Sprite(texture);
```

If you ever need to know what the resolution of a loaded texture is, you can find out by using texture's `baseTexture.resolution` property (`anySprite.texture.baseTexture.resolution`).

Rope Mesh

Another fun effect is a **rope mesh**. It allows you to make a sprite oscillate like a wave or slither like a snake, as shown in Figure 6-11.

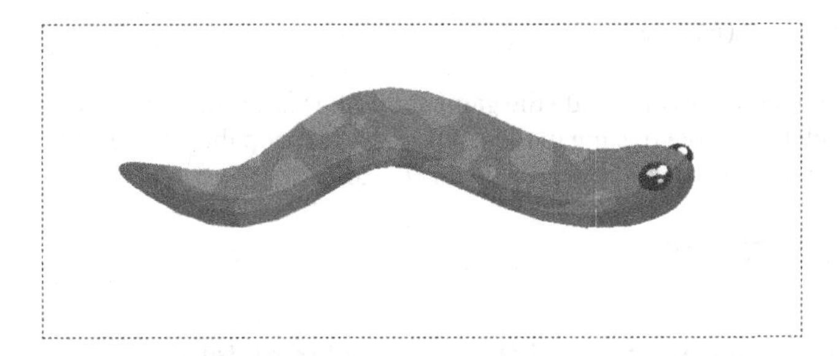

Figure 6-11. *Creating a wave effect with a rope mesh*

First, start with an image of the thing you want to deform. The slithering snake actually started as a plain, straight-line image, shown in Figure 6-12.

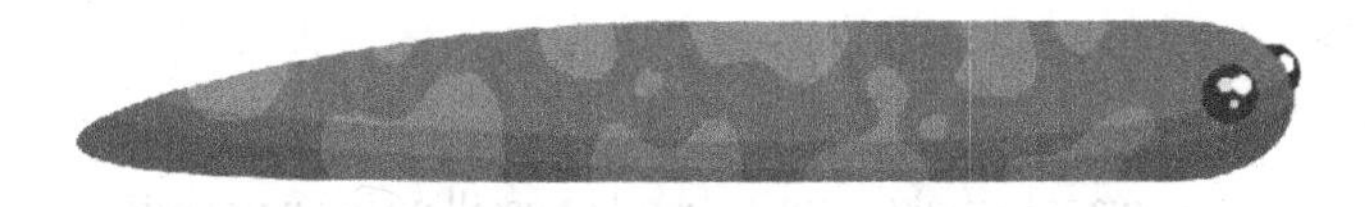

Figure 6-12. *Starting with a straight-line image*

Then decide how many segments along the snake you want to move independently. The snake image is 600 pixels wide, so about 20 segments would create a nice effect. Divide the image width by the number of segments, to find the length of each rope segment.

```
numberOfSegments = 20;
imageWidth = 600;
ropeSegment = imageWidth / numberOfSegments;
```

Next, create an array of 20 `Point` objects. Each point's x position (the first argument) will be separated from the next point by a distance of one `ropeSegment`.

```
points = [];
for (let i = 0; i < numberOfSegments; i++) {
  points.push(new Point(i * ropeSegment, 0));
}
```

Now create a new Rope object (`PIXI.mesh.Rope`). Supply two arguments: the image texture and the `points` array.

```
let snake = new Rope(TextureCache["images/snake.png"], points);
```

Add the snake to a parent container, so that it's a bit easier to position. Then add the container to the stage and position it.

```
let snakeContainer = new Container();
snakeContainer.addChild(snake);
stage.addChild(snakeContainer);
snakeContainer.position.set(64, 128);
```

Now you have to animate the points inside the game loop (the `play` function, in the application structure model we've been using in this book). The `for` loop that creates the wave effect works by moving each point of the array in an ellipse.

```
//Increment the counter each frame
counter += 0.1;

//Loop through all the points and shift them in a circular pattern
//to produce the rippling effect
for (let i = 0; i < points.length; i++) {
  points[i].y = Math.sin((i * 0.5) + counter) * 30;
  points[i].x
    = i * ropeSegment
    + Math.cos((i * 0.3) + counter)
    * numberOfSegments;
}
```

Use a rope mesh anytime you want to make a sprite bend or oscillate in an organic and very natural-looking way.

Tweening and Transitions

You've learned two ways to animate sprites in this book so far: moving them programmatically with code and using keyframe animation. But there's a third way: **tweening**! A **tween** is a quick, pre-baked animation effect that you can apply to a sprite with a single line of code, to make it change its position, scale, or alpha. You set the start and end values, and the tween automatically fills in all the in-between states.

■ **Note** If you haven't already guessed, the term *tween* comes from *in-between*.

Pixi doesn't have its own built-in tweening engine, but there are plenty of good open source, general purpose tweening libraries that you can use, including Tween.js and Dynamic.js. Use either of those two libraries, if you want to make very specialized custom tween effects. But I'm going to show you a very easy-to-use one called Charm.js, which was made by me and designed to work specifically with Pixi.

Setting Up and Running Charm

To start using Charm, download it from its code repository (`github.com/kittykatattack/charm`) and link to the `charm.js` file with a `<script>` tag. Create a new instance of Charm at the beginning of your program and initialize it using the `PIXI` object in the constructor, as follows:

```
c = new Charm(PIXI);
```

The variable `c` now represents our running instance of Charm.

Just as with the particle effects you learned to use in the previous chapter, tweens must be updated for each frame in the game loop. Call Charm's `update` method in the game loop, just after you call the `state` function, as follows:

```
function gameLoop(){
  requestAnimationFrame(gameLoop);
  state();
  c.update();
  renderer.render(stage);
}
```

Now you're ready to start tweening!

Sliding Tweens

One of Charm's most useful tween effects is `slide`. Use the `slide` method to make a sprite move smoothly from its current position on the canvas to any other position. The `slide` method takes seven arguments, but only the first three are required.

```
slide(
  anySprite,              //A sprite
  finalXPosition,         //The x position where the movement should end
  finalYPosition,         //The y position where the movement should end
  durationInFrames,       //How long the movement should last, in frames
  easingType,             //The easing style of the movement
  yoyo?,                  //A Boolean. Should the sprite yoyo?
  delayTimeBeforeRepeat   //Delay time, in ms, before the sprite yoyos.
)
```

`durationInFrames` determines the number of frames over which the tween should occur (the default is 60). The `easingType` is a string that can be any of 15 different types, which you'll find listed ahead (the default is `"smoothstep"`). yoyo is a Boolean that determines whether the sprite should move back and forth continuously between the tween's start and end points. `delayTimeBeforeRepeat` is a number, in milliseconds, that determines the amount of optional delay before the sprite yoyos back.

Here's how to use the `slide` method to make a sprite move from its original position to x/y point 128/128 over 120 frames. Figure 6-13 illustrates the effect.

```
c.slide(pixie, 128, 128, 120);
```

Figure 6-13. *Sliding a sprite to a new position*

That's the only line of code you have to write. Charm's engine animates the sprite automatically for you. This code will work the same way in the `setup` function or in your game loop (the `play` function). If you want the sprite to yoyo back and forth between its start and end points, here's some code you could write:

```
c.slide(pixie, 128, 128, 120, "smoothstep", true);
```

`true` turns the yoyo effect on.

Tween Objects

All of Charm's tween methods return a `tween` object, which you can create like this:

```
let slidePixie = c.slide(pixie, 128, 128, 120);
```

`slidePixie` is the tween object in this example, and it contains some useful properties and methods that let you control the tween.

One of these is a user-assignable `onComplete` method that will run as soon as the tween is finished. Here's how you could use `onComplete` to display a message in the console when the sprite has reached its destination.

```
let slidePixie = c.slide(pixie, 128, 128, 120);
slidePixie.onComplete = () => console.log("Pixie slide complete");
```

If you set yoyo to `true`, `onComplete` will run continuously whenever the sprite reaches both its start and end points.

Tweens also have `pause` and `play` methods that let you stop and start the tween.

```
slidePixie.pause();
slidePixie.play();
```

Tween objects have a `playing` property that will be `true` if the tween is currently playing. All of Charm's methods return tween objects that you can control and access similarly.

Setting the Easing Types

The `slide` method's fourth argument is the `easingType`. It's a string that determines how quickly or slowly the tween speeds up and slows down. There are 15 of these types to choose from, and they're the same for all of Charm's different tween methods. The easing types fall in to 5 general categories, so you can pick one by first choosing the general category and then the more specific type. Each category has a basic type and then a `squared` and cubed version. The squared and cubed versions just exaggerate the basic effect to further degrees. The default easing type for most of Charm's tweens is "smoothstep".

- **Linear**: "linear". No easing on the sprite at all; the sprite just starts and stops abruptly
- **Smoothstep**: "smoothstep", "smoothstepSquared", "smoothstepCubed". Speeds the sprite up and slows it down in a very natural looking way
- **Acceleration**: "acceleration", "accelerationCubed". Gradually speeds the sprite up and stops it abruptly. For a slightly more rounded acceleration effect, use "sine", "sineSquared", or "sineCubed".
- **Deceleration**: "deceleration", "decelerationCubed". Starts the sprite abruptly and gradually slows it down. For a slightly more rounded deceleration effect, use "inverseSine", "inverseSineSquared", or "inverseSineCubed".
- **Bounce**: "bounce 10 -10". This will make the sprite overshoot the start and end points and bounce slightly when it hits them. Try changing the multipliers, 10 and -10, to vary the effect.

Use any of these easing types in Charm's tween methods in the examples that follow.

Using slide for Scene Transitions

One thing you'll definitely want to do in your game or application is make a screen slide away and a new screen slide into view. It could be your game's title screen that slides away to reveal the game's first level, or it could be a menu screen that slides away to reveal more application content. You can use the slide method to do this. A quick practical example will demonstrate how.

First, create two container objects: sceneOne and sceneTwo and add them to the stage.

```
sceneOne = new Container();
sceneTwo = new Container();
stage.addChild(sceneOne);
stage.addChild(sceneTwo);
```

Next, create sprites for each scene. Make a blue rectangle as big as the canvas; make some text that displays "Scene One"; and add both to the sceneOne container. Make a red rectangle as big as the canvas; make some text that displays "Scene Two"; and add both of those to the sceneTwo container. You'll end up with two container objects that might look something like what you see in Figure 6-14.

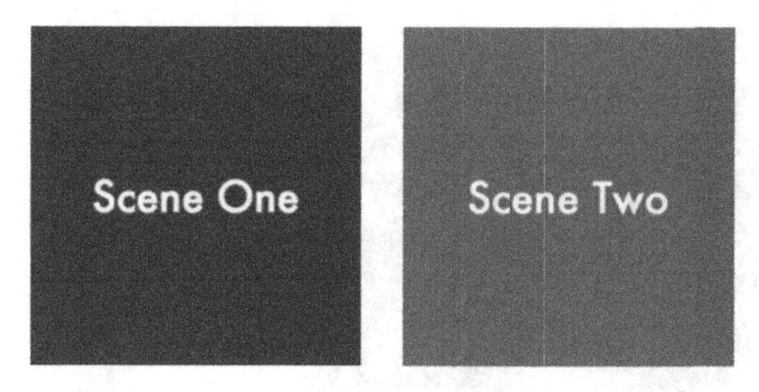

Figure 6-14. *Two containers that represent each scene*

Here's an abridged version of some code that you could write to do this:

```
//1. Scene one sprites:

let blueRectangle = new Graphics();
//... draw the rectangle ...
sceneOne.addChild(blueRectangle);

let sceneOneText = new Text(/*...*/);
//... format the text and center it ...
sceneOne.addChild(sceneOneText);

//2. Scene two sprites:

let redRectangle = new Graphics();
//... draw the rectangle ...
sceneTwo.addChild(redRectangle);

let sceneTwoText = new Text(/*...*/);
//... format the text and center it ...
sceneTwo.addChild(sceneTwoText);
```

Of course, in a real project, you would fill each container with as many sprites as you require for each scene, just as we did in the Treasure Hunter game in Chapter 4. You can add as many more scene containers as you need for your project.

Next, move `sceneTwo` out of the way, so that it's sitting beyond the right edge of the canvas. A line of code such as the following will do the trick:

```
sceneTwo.x = renderer.width;
```

This will reveal `sceneOne` on the canvas, with `sceneTwo` waiting to slide out from the left when it's needed. Figure 6-15 illustrates this.

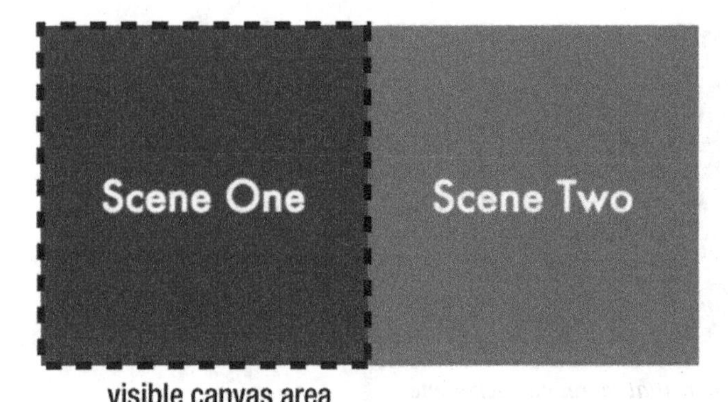

Figure 6-15. *sceneTwo is waiting just offscreen*

Finally, use the `slide` method to transition from `sceneOne` to `sceneTwo`. Just slide `sceneOne` out of the way, to the left, and slide `sceneTwo` in from the right, to take its place.

```
c.slide(sceneTwo, 0, 0);
c.slide(sceneOne, -renderer.width, 0);
```

Figure 6-16 illustrates what this code will do.

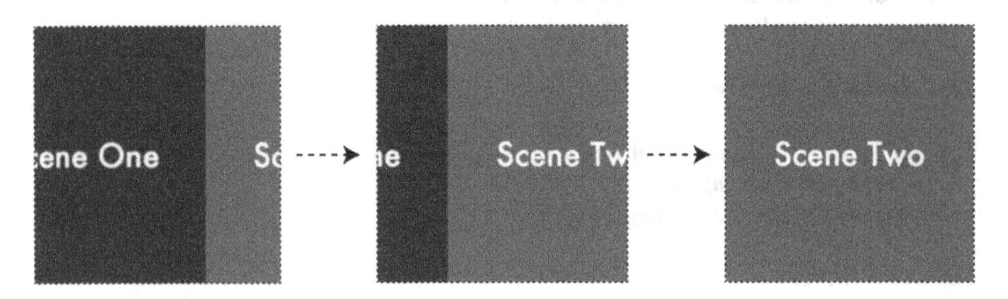

Figure 6-16. *A smooth transition from scene one to scene two*

Timed Transitions

You can initiate a transition like this in your game and application whenever you need it. You can make the transition occur after a set time interval, by using a helpful custom function called `wait`.

```
function wait(duration = 0) {
  return new Promise((resolve, reject) => {
    setTimeout(resolve, duration);
  });
}
```

To use wait, supply its one argument with the time, in milliseconds, that you want it to wait for. Here's how you can use wait to transition from sceneOne to sceneTwo after a delay of 1 second (1000 milliseconds).

```
wait(1000).then(() => {
  c.slide(sceneTwo, 0, 0);
  c.slide(sceneOne, -renderer.width, 0);
});
```

In the next chapter, you'll learn how to use mouse and touch interaction, which you can use to initiate actions such as this.

Following Curves

The slide method animates a sprite along a straight line, but you can use another method, called followCurve, to make a sprite move along a Bezier curve. First, define the Bezier curve as a 2D array of 4 x/y points, as follows:

```
let curve = [
  [pixie.x, pixie.y],      //Start position
  [108, 32],               //Control point 1
  [176, 32],               //Control point 2
  [196, 160]               //End position
];
```

The second and third set of points are the Bezier curve's control points (see Chapter 3, if you need a reminder of how Bezier curve control points work). Next, use Charm's followCurve method to make a sprite follow that curve. (Supply the curve array as the second argument.)

```
c.followCurve(
  pixie,               //The sprite
  curve,               //The Bezier curve array
  120,                 //Duration, in milliseconds
  "smoothstep",        //Easing type
  true,                //Should the tween yoyo?
  1000                 //Delay, in milliseconds, before it yoyos
);
```

Only the first two arguments are required. Figure 6-17 illustrates the effect.

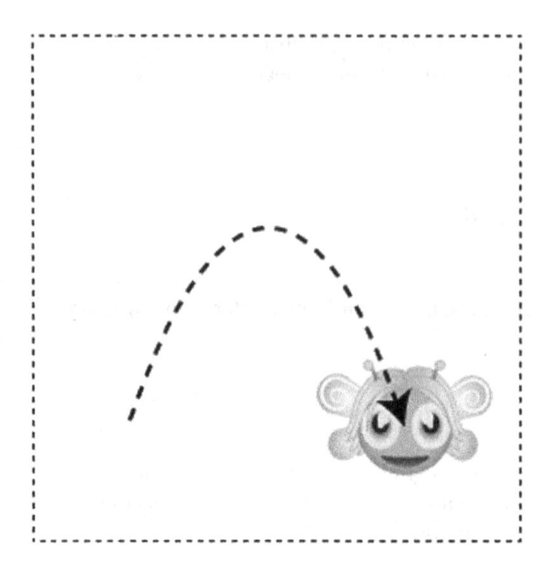

Figure 6-17. *Making a sprite follow a curve*

You'll have the best result if you center the sprite over the curve. You can do that by centering the sprite's anchor point, as follows:

```
pixie.anchor.set(0.5, 0.5);
```

The `slide` and `followCurve` methods are good for simple back-and-forth animation effects, but you can also connect them to make sprites traverse complex paths.

Following Paths

You can use Charm's `walkPath` method to connect a series of points and make a sprite move to each of those points. Each point in the series is called a `waypoint`. First, start with a 2D array of x/y position waypoints that map out the path you want the sprite to follow.

```
let waypoints = [
  [32, 32],          //First x/y point
  [32, 128],         //Next x/y point
  [300, 128],        //Next x/y point
  [300, 32],         //Next x/y point
  [32, 32]           //Last x/y point
];
```

You can use as many waypoints as you need.

Next, use the walkPath method to make the sprite move to all those points, in sequence. (Only the first two arguments are required.)

```
c.walkPath(
  cat,                //The sprite
  waypoints,          //The array of waypoints
  300,                //Total duration, in frames
  "smoothstep",       //Easing type
  true,               //Should the path loop?
  true,               //Should the path reverse?
  1000                //Delay in milliseconds between segments
);
```

If you set the fifth argument to true, the sprite will start again from the beginning when it reaches the end. If you set the sixth argument to true, the sprite will walk the path in reverse when it reaches the end. The last argument sets the delay, in milliseconds, that the sprite should wait before moving to the next section of the path. Figure 6-18 illustrates what this code does.

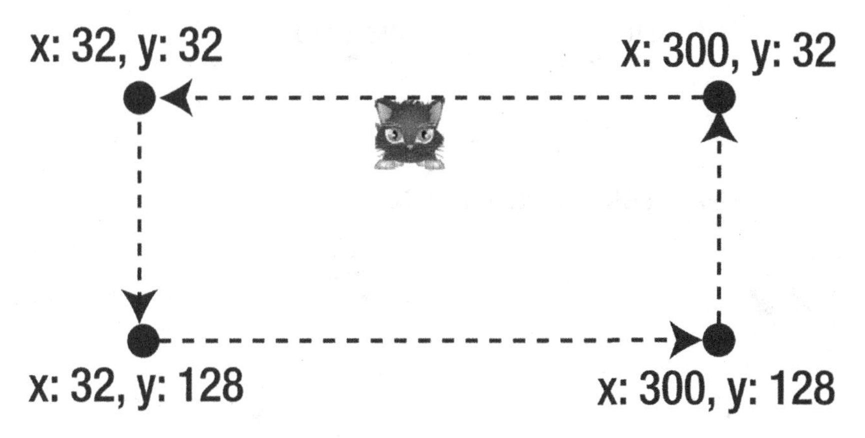

Figure 6-18. *Making a sprite follow a path of connected waypoints*

With the walkCurve method, you can make a sprite follow a series of connected curves. First, create any array of Bezier curves that describe the path you want the sprite to follow.

```
let curvedWaypoints = [

    //First curve
    [[hedgehog.x, hedgehog.y],[75, 500],[200, 500],[300, 300]],

    //Second curve
    [[300, 300],[250, 100],[100, 100],[hedgehog.x, hedgehog.y]]
];
```

The four points for each curve are the same as in the `followCurve` method: the start position, control point 1, control point 2, and the end position. The last point in the first curve should be the same as the first point in the next curve. You can use as many curves as you need.

Next, supply the `curvedWaypoints` array as the second argument in the `walkCurve` method:

```
let hedgehogPath = c.walkCurve(
  hedgehog,                     //The sprite
  curvedWaypoints,              //Array of curved waypoints
  300,                          //Total duration, in frames
  "smoothstep",                 //Easing type
  true,                         //Should the path loop?
  true,                         //Should the path yoyo?
  1000                          //Delay in milliseconds between segments
);
```

Figure 6-19 illustrates the effect of this code.

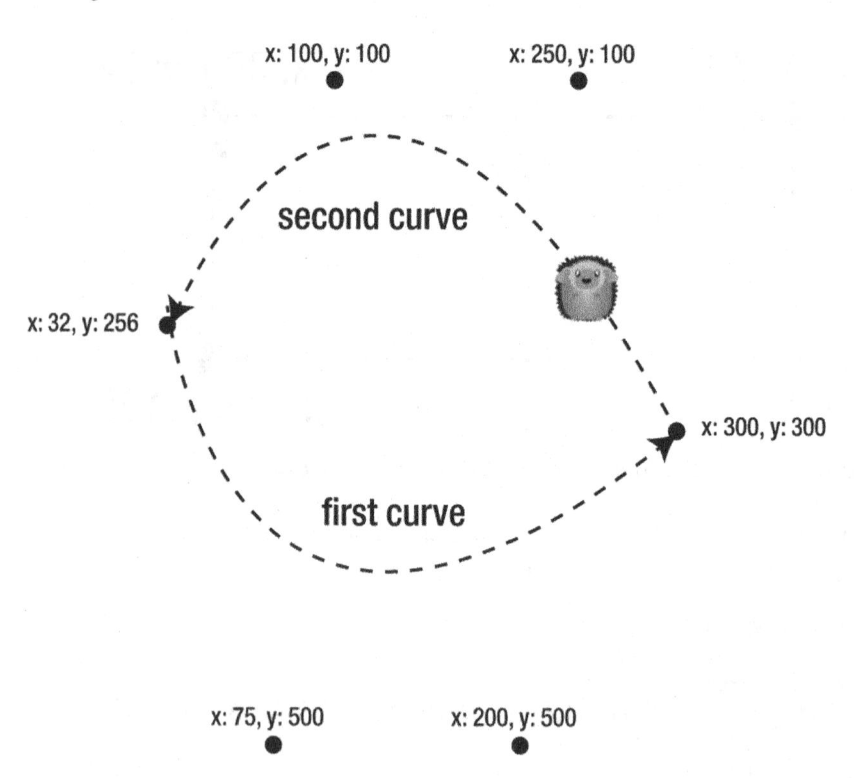

Figure 6-19. *Making a sprite follow a path of connected curves*

Using walkPath and walkCurve will give you a great head start for making some fun animated sprites for games.

A Few More Tween Effects

Charm has bunch of other built-in tween effects that you'll find a lot of use for in games and applications. Here's a quick roundup.

fadeOut and fadeIn

Use fadeOut to make a sprite become gradually transparent and fadeIn to make it reappear. Here's their most basic usage:

```
c.fadeOut(anySprite);
c.fadeIn(anySprite);
```

The optional second argument is the duration, in frames, that the fade should last (the default is 60 frames).

pulse

Use pulse to make a sprite fade out and in, continuously, at a steady rate.

```
c.pulse(anySprite);
```

The optional second argument is the duration, in frames, between each fade-in and fade-out. An optional third argument lets you set the minimum alpha level that the sprite should be reduced to. For example, if you only want the sprite to become half-transparent before fading in again, set the third argument to 0.5, as follows:

```
c.pulse(anySprite, 60, 0.5);
```

scale

You can tween a sprite's scale with the scale method. Here are the arguments you can use (only the first is required):

```
c.scale(
  anySprite          //The sprite
  endScaleX,         //The final x scale value
  endScaleY,         //The final y scale value
  durationInframes   //The duration, in frames
);
```

breathe

If you want the scale tween effect to yoyo back and forth, use the related breathe method. It's a scaling effect that makes a sprite look as though it's breathing in and out. Here's the full argument list (only the first is required):

```
c.breathe(
  anySprite,           //The sprite
  endScaleX,           //The final scale x value
  endScaleY,           //The final scale y value
  frames,              //The duration, in frames
  yoyo,                //Should the tween yoyo?
  delayBeforeRepeat,   //Delay, in milliseconds, before yoyoing
);
```

strobe

Use the strobe method to make a sprite appear to flash like a strobe light, by rapidly changing its scale.

```
c.strobe(sprite);
```

wobble

Make a sprite wobble like a plate of jelly, using the wobble method.

```
c.wobble(sprite);
```

If you use any of these scaling tween effects (scale, breathe, strobe, or wobble), center the sprite's anchor point, so that the scaling occurs from the sprite's center.

Summary

In this chapter, we overturned Pixi's toy box on the floor and spent a dizzying few pages playing with all the contents. You learned how to make infinite scrolling effects with tiling sprites, slithering snakes with rope meshes, and how to display videos on sprites. You also learned everything you need to know about manipulating textures with cacheAsBitmap, generateTexture, and RenderTexture. If that's not enough, you found out how to tint sprites, use masks, transparency blend modes, as well as Pixi's vast collection of filter effects. And, finally, you learned how to quickly create scene transition and sprite easing effects with the Charm micro-library.

Are you exhausted yet? No? That's great, because there's one more exciting chapter just around the corner! It will cover the last essential skill you have to know to start working with Pixi: mouse and touch interactivity.

CHAPTER 7

Mouse and Touch Events

You've learned how to add interactivity to sprites, using the keyboard, but most of your games and applications will use a mouse or touch interface. In this chapter, you'll learn how to

- Use a universal pointer object to interact with sprites
- Work with mouse and touch events
- Create a drag-and-drop interface
- Create clickable, pressable buttons

And, as a bonus, at the end of this chapter, you'll put all these skills together to make a complete game.

But first, let's find out the basics you need to know to start using mouse and touch interactivity with Pixi.

Setting Up Tink

Pixi has a limited set of built-in tools for mouse and touch interactivity, but for the kinds of rich interactivity you'll need for games and applications, I recommend that you use a third-party library to make things easier. I wrote a lightweight helper library called Tink that adds some of the most useful features you'll need: a universal pointer object, a drag-and-drop interface, and a `button` object.

To start using Tink, first download it from its source code repository: `github.com/kittykatattack/tink`. Link to the tink.js script in your HTML file, and create a new instance of Tink at the beginning of your program. Supply it with a reference to PIXI and the `renderer.view` object (the HTML5 canvas).

```
let t = new Tink(PIXI, renderer.view);
```

(In this chapter, the variable `t` will represent our running Tink instance.) Generally, you should create a new Tink instance in your `setup` function, after all the resources have loaded.

Next, call Tink's update method inside your game loop, to update all of Tink's interactive objects each frame. In the application template model we've been using in this book, update Tink just after you call the state function, as follows:

```
function gameLoop(){
  requestAnimationFrame(gameLoop);
  state();
  t.update();
  renderer.render(stage);
}
```

This is what you need to get started on the examples in the chapter.

■ **Note** Among its many other helpful methods that you'll learn ahead, Tink also includes the keyboard method that you learned to use in Chapter 2 to capture key presses.

Setting the Optional Scale

Tink's constructor has an optional second argument: scale. The default scale value is 1, but if you've rescaled the canvas using the scaleToWindow function you learned to use in Chapter 1, supply scaleToWindow's return value. Here's an example of what this might look like:

First, run scaleToWindow and capture the returned scale value at the beginning of your program.

```
let scale = scaleToWindow(renderer.view);
```

Next, create a new instance of Tink in the setup function, and supply the scale value as the second argument in the constructor.

```
let t = new Tink(PIXI, renderer.view, scale);
```

This will ensure that the coordinates that Tink uses will match the canvas's scaled pixel coordinates.

A Universal Pointer

Tink lets you make a pointer object that automatically figures out whether the user is interacting with a mouse or with touch. Use Tink's makePointer method to create a pointer.

```
pointer = t.makePointer();
```

Usually, one pointer will be enough for most games or applications, but you can make as many as you require.

■ **Note** Does your game or application require complex multi-touch interaction with gestures? Then consider using an excellent HTML5 library called hammer.js (`hammerjs.github.io/getting-started/`).

The `pointer` object has three user-definable methods that you can program: `press`, `release`, and `tap`. `press` is triggered when the left mouse button is pressed, or the user presses his or her finger to the device screen. `release` is triggered when the mouse button is released, or the user lifts his or her finger from the screen. `tap` is triggered if the left mouse button is clicked, or the user taps the screen. Here's an example of how you can define these methods on the `pointer`:

```
pointer.press = () => console.log("The pointer was pressed");
pointer.release = () => console.log("The pointer was released");
pointer.tap = () => console.log("The pointer was tapped");
```

Also use the `tap` method to capture mouse clicks.

The pointer also has `x` and `y` properties that tell you its position on the canvas (Pixi's `renderer.view`).

```
pointer.x
pointer.y
```

It also has three Boolean properties that indicate the pointer's current state: `isUp`, `isDown`, and `tapped`.

```
pointer.isUp
pointer.isDown
pointer.tapped
```

■ **Note** Run the `pointer.html` file in this chapter's source files, for an interactive demonstration of how to create and use a pointer.

Pointer Interaction with Sprites

The `pointer` has a `hitTestSprite` method that you can use to find out if the pointer is touching a sprite.

```
pointer.hitTestSprite(anySprite);
```

If the `pointer` is within the rectangular area of a sprite, `hitTestSprite` will return `true`.

hitTestSprite will also work with circular sprites. Just add a property called circular to a sprite and set it to true.

```
anyCircularSprite.circular = true;
```

This flags hitTestSprite to use a circular collision detection algorithm instead of the default rectangular one.

If you want to display a hand icon while the pointer is over a sprite, you can set the pointer's cursor property to "pointer". Setting it to "auto" when the pointer leaves the sprite's area will display the default arrow icon. Following is some sample code you could use inside your game loop to enable this feature:

```
if (pointer.hitTestSprite(anySprite)) {

  //Display a hand icon while the pointer is over the sprite
  pointer.cursor = "pointer";
}
else {

  //Display the default arrow icon when the
  //pointer moves outside the sprite's area
  pointer.cursor = "auto";
}
```

■ **Note** pointer.cursor only references the HTML5 canvas element's style.cursor property to achieve this, using two standard values from the HTML5 spec: "pointer" and "auto". You can assign any cursor style value that you like. (A web search for "HTML style cursor" will turn up a complete list of possible values.) You can also set this manually, if you want to through Pixi's renderer.view object. Here's how: renderer.view.style.cursor = "cursorStyle".

These cursor styles will only be visible on a mouse-based interface; on a touch interface, they're ignored.

Run the spriteInteractivity.html file in the chapter's source files for a working example, shown in Figure 7-1.

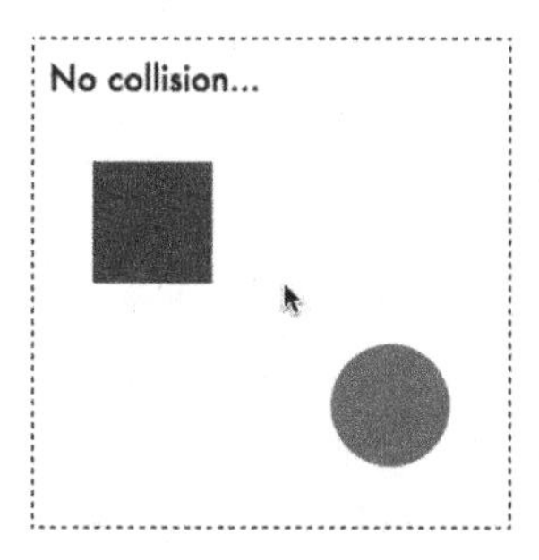

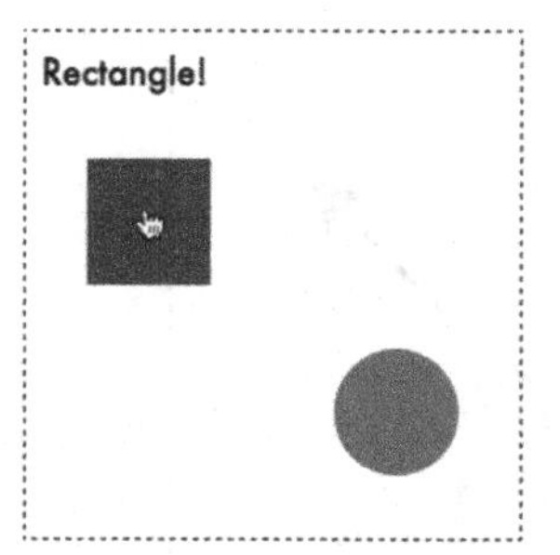

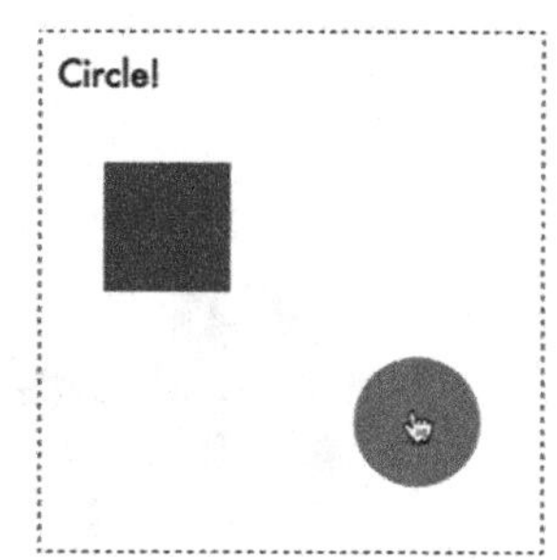

Figure 7-1. *Interacting with sprites by using a pointer*

Move the pointer over the square and circle sprites and watch how the cursor icon changes. The text also displays "Rectangle!" or "Circle!" or "No collision...," based on what the pointer is touching. Because the circle sprite's `circular` property was set to `true`, you'll notice that the shape of the circle is accurately detected. Here's the code from the game loop that achieves these effects:

```
if (pointer.hitTestSprite(rectangle)) {
  message.text = "Box!";
  pointer.cursor = "pointer";
}
else if (pointer.hitTestSprite(circle)) {
  message.text = "Circle!";
  pointer.cursor = "pointer";
}
else {
  message.text = "No collision...";
  pointer.cursor = "auto";
}
```

Being able to detect which sprite the pointer is touching is nice, but better still would be if you could use it to move the sprite around the canvas. You can!

Drag-and-Drop Sprites

You can add drag-and-drop functionality to a sprite with Tink's `makeDraggable` method. Just supply it with a single sprite, or a list of sprites, that you want to make draggable.

```
t.makeDraggable(cat, tiger, hedgehog);
```

You can then use the mouse or touch to drag the sprites around the canvas, as shown in Figure 7-2.

Figure 7-2. *Using the `makeDraggable` method to drag sprites around the canvas*

When you select a draggable sprite, its stacking order changes so that it appears above the other sprites. The mouse's arrow icon also changes to a hand when it's over a draggable sprite.

Draggable sprites have a Boolean property called `draggable` that is set to `true`. To disable dragging, set `draggable` to `false`.

```
anySprite.draggable = false;
```

Setting it back to `true` will enable dragging again.

To completely remove a sprite (or list of sprites) from the drag-and-drop system, use the `makeUndraggable` method, as follows:

```
t.makeUndraggable(cat, tiger, hedgehog);
```

Drag-and-drop is a fundamental interactive feature that can be used as the basis for making puzzles, games, matching games, or sophisticated user interfaces.

■ **Note** If you're making a drag-and-drop matching game, use the `hitTestRectangle` function you learned in Chapter 4, to find out whether a sprite you're dragging is touching the correct destination target sprite.

Buttons

Buttons are an important user interface (UI) component that you'll definitely want to use in your games and applications. Tink has a useful `button` method that lets you quickly create them. Before I show you how to make buttons, let's first find out what buttons actually are and how you can use them.

What Are Buttons?

You can think of buttons as "clickable/touchable sprites." The most important thing you have to know about buttons is that they have **states** and **actions**. States define what the button looks like, and actions define what it does.

Most buttons have the following three states:

- **Up**. When the pointer is not touching the button
- **Over**. When the pointer is over the button
- **Down**. When the pointer is pressing down on the button.
  Figure 7-3 shows an example of these three button states.

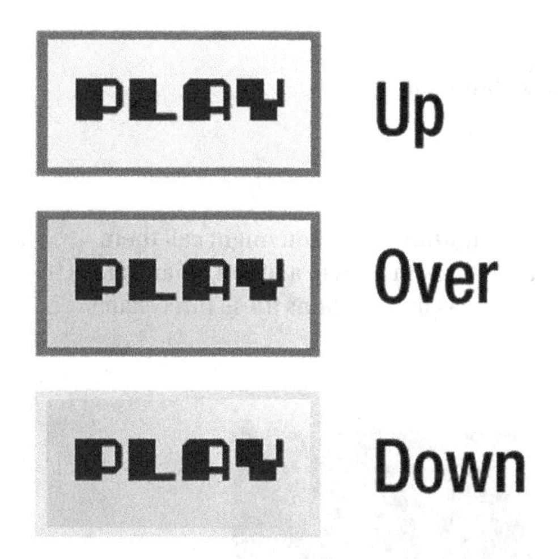

Figure 7-3. *Up, Over, and Down button states*

Touch-based interfaces require only two states: up and down.

With the button object that you'll learn to make in the next section, you will be able to access these states through the button's `state` property, as follows:

```
playButton.state
```

The `state` property could have the string value `"up"`, `"over"`, or `"down"`, which you could use in your game logic.

Buttons also have **actions**, such as the following:

- **Press**. When the pointer presses the button
- **Release**. When the pointer is released from the button
- **Over**. When the pointer moves into the button's area.
- **Out**. When the pointer moves out of the button's area
- **Tap**. When the button has been tapped (or clicked)

You can define these actions as user-definable methods, like this:

```
playButton.press = () => console.log("pressed");
playButton.release = () => console.log("released");
playButton.over = () => console.log("over");
playButton.out = () => console.log("out");
playButton.tap = () => console.log("tapped");
```

In the button object that we'll make ahead, you'll be able to access the button's "pressed" and "released" actions in a string property, as follows:

```
playButton.action
```

Got it? Good! So, how do we actually make buttons?

Making Buttons

First, start with three images that define the three button states. You might call them `up.png`, `over.png`, and `down.png`. Then add those three images to a tileset, or as frames in a texture atlas. Figure 7-4 shows a simple texture atlas that contains these three states.

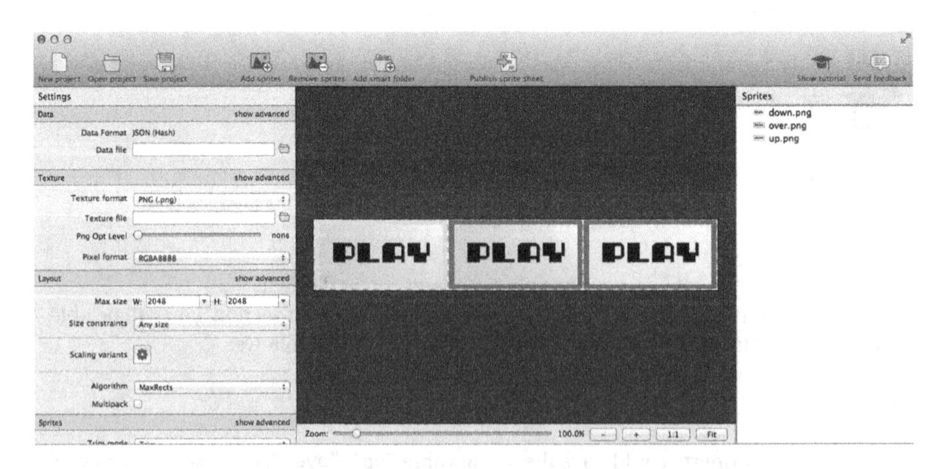

***Figure 7-4.** Adding the button image states to a texture atlas*

■ **Note** Although having three image states is standard, sometimes buttons have only two image states. This is particularly true of touch-only buttons, which don't have an "over" state. The button object that we're going to make will use three images, if they're available, but if there are only two, they will be used for the "up" and "down" states.

Next, publish the texture atlas and load it into your program.

```
loader
  .add("images/button.json")
  .load(setup);
```

Then, in the `setup` function where you initialize your sprites, create an array that references each of the three button frames in this order: up, over, and down.

```
let buttonFrames = [
  id["up.png"],
  id["over.png"],
  id["down.png"]
];
```

These don't have to be frame ids: you can use an array of any Pixi textures, such as single image textures, if you want to.

Finally, use Tink's `button` method to create the button. Supply the `buttonFrames` array as the first argument.

```
let playButton = t.button(buttonFrames, 32, 96);
```

The second and third optional arguments are the button's x and y position.

And don't forget to add the button to `stage`!

```
stage.addChild(playButton);
```

At its heart, a button is just an ordinary Pixi `MovieClip` with extra properties and methods, so you can treat it like any other `MovieClip`.

To see this button in action, run the `button.html` file in this chapter's source code files. Its output is shown in Figure 7-5. When you move the pointer over the button, the cursor changes to a hand icon. The game loop updates some text that displays the button's state and action.

```
stateMessage.text = `State: ${playButton.state}`;
actionMessage.text = `Action: ${playButton.action}`;
```

No interaction

State: over
Action:
PLAY

The pointer moves over the button

The pointer presses down on the button

The pointer is released

Figure 7-5. *An interactive button sprite*

And now you have an essential UI element that you can use in all kinds of games and applications.

Making an Interactive Sprite

Tink has another useful method called makeInteractive that lets you add button properties and methods to any ordinary sprite.

```
t.makeInteractive(anySprite);
```

This lets you turn any sprite into a button-like object. You can now assign press or release methods to the sprite and access its state and action properties, as follows:

```
anySprite.press = () => {
  //Do something when the pointer presses the sprite
};

anySprite.release = () => {
  //Do something when the pointer is released after pressing the sprite
};
```

Take a look at the interactiveSprite.html file in the chapter's source files for an example of how you could use this feature to make a shape that randomly changes color each time you press it. (See Figure 7-6.)

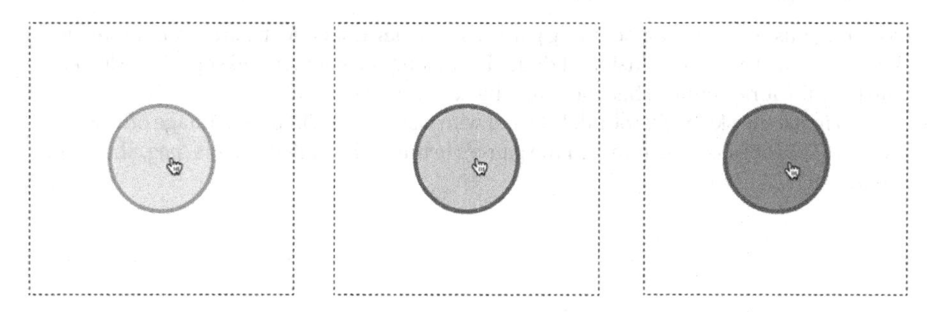

Figure 7-6. *Clicking to make the circle display random colors*

Now that you know how to add interactivity to any sprite, let's find out how you can use this new skill to make a game.

Case Study: Pixie Perilousness!

Play the game Pixie Perilousness! in this chapter's source files (pixiePerilousness.html) for a great example of a simple game that you can make using most of the tools you've learned in this book. Tap the screen to make the pixie fly, and help her navigate through the gaps in 15 pillars to reach the finish, as shown in Figure 7-7. A trail of multicolored fairy dust follows her as she flies through the course. If she hits one of the green blocks, she explodes in a shower of dust. But if she manages to navigate through the increasingly narrowing gaps between all 15 pillars, she reaches a big floating "Finish" sign.

Figure 7-7. *Helping the pixie fly through the obstacle course of pillars to reach the finish*

The game is less than 300 lines of code long and is a great model for you to use to start building your own games. Let's go on a quick tour of how Pixie Perilousness! was made.

■ **Note** You'll find the complete source code listing for Pixie Perilousness! in Appendix A, which you can use as a reference to see how all the code fits together in its proper context.

Creating the Scrolling Background

Pixie Perilousness! is a side-scrolling game using a **parallax** effect. Parallax is a shallow 3D effect that creates the illusion of depth by making the background scroll at a slower rate than the foreground. This makes the background look as if it's farther away.

To make the sky background, I started with a seamless 512 by 512 image of some clouds. The image is a big frame in the game's texture atlas called `clouds.png`, shown in Figure 7-8.

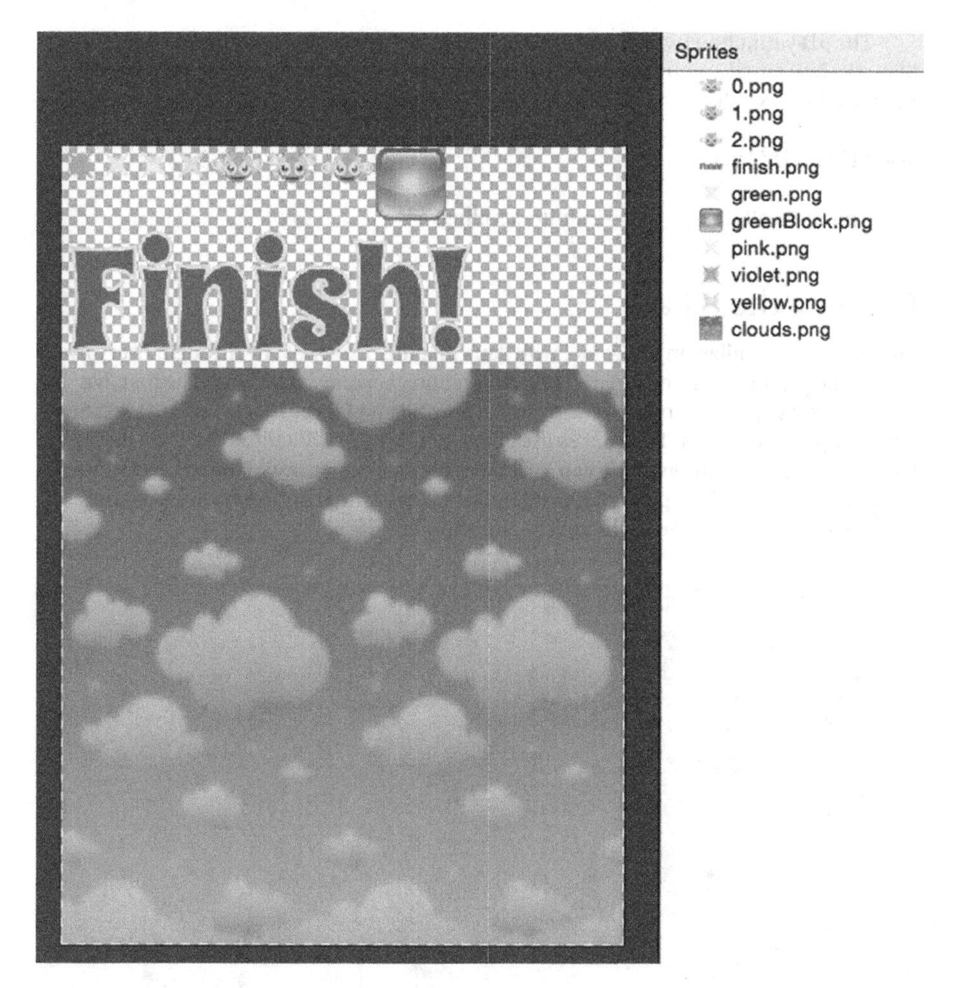

Figure 7-8. *The `clouds.png` frame image in the texture atlas*

In the program's `setup` function, I used the `clouds.png` frame to create a `TilingSprite` called sky.

```
sky = new TilingSprite(
  id["clouds.png"],
  renderer.view.width,
  renderer.view.height
);
stage.addChild(sky);
```

The `play` function (which is called each frame by `gameLoop`) then moves the tiling sky by a small amount to the left of each frame, by slightly decreasing the sky's `tilePosition.x` value.

```
sky.tilePosition.x -= 1;
```

And that's all there is to it—infinite scrolling!

Creating the Pillars

There are fifteen pillars in the game, with gaps that the pixie must fly through. Every five pillars, the gap between the top and bottom sections becomes narrower. The first five pillars have a gap of four blocks, the next five have a gap of three blocks, and the last five have a gap of two blocks. This makes the game increasingly difficult as the pixie flies farther. The exact position of the gap is random for each pillar, and different every time the game is played. Each pillar is spaced by 384 pixels, but Figure 7-9 shows what they would look like if they were right next to one another.

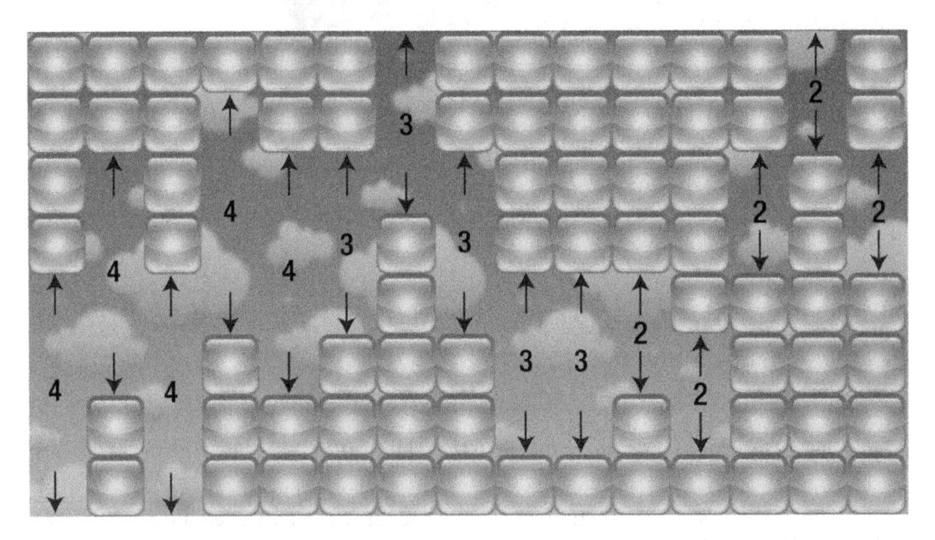

***Figure 7-9.** The gap between the top and bottom of each pillar gradually narrows*

You can see how the gap gradually narrows from four spaces on the left down to two on the right.

All the blocks that make up the pillars are in a `Container` called blocks.

```
blocks = new Container();
stage.addChild(blocks);
```

A nested for loop creates each block and adds it to the blocks container. The outer loop runs fifteen times, once to create each pillar. The inner loop runs eight times, once for each block in the pillar. The blocks are only added if they're not occupying the range that's been randomly chosen for the gap. Every fifth time the outer loop runs, the size of the gap narrows by one. All this happens inside the program's setup function.

```
//What should the initial size of the gap be between the pillars?
let gapSize = 4;

//How many pillars?
let numberOfPillars = 15;

//Loop 15 times to make 15 pillars
for (let i = 0; i < numberOfPillars; i++) {

  //Randomly place the gap somewhere inside the pillar
  let startGapNumber = randomInt(0, 8 - gapSize);

  //Reduce the `gapSize` by one after every fifth pillar. This is
  //what makes gaps gradually become narrower
  if (i > 0 && i % 5 === 0) gapSize -= 1;

  //Create a block if it's not within the range of numbers
  //occupied by the gap
  for (let j = 0; j < 8; j++) {
    if (j < startGapNumber || j > startGapNumber + gapSize - 1) {
      let block = u.sprite(id["greenBlock.png"]);
      blocks.addChild(block);

      //Space each pillar 384 pixels apart. The first pillar will be
      //placed at an x position of 512
      block.x = (i * 384) + 512;
      block.y = j * 64;
    }
  }

  //After the pillars have been created, add the finish image
  //right at the end
  if (i === numberOfPillars - 1) {
    finish = u.sprite(id["finish.png"]);
    blocks.addChild(finish);
    finish.x = (i * 384) + 896;
    finish.y = 192;
  }
}
```

The last part of the code adds the big floating finish sprite to the world, which the pixie will see, if she manages to make it through to the end.

The play function moves the group of blocks by 2 pixels to the right each frame, but only while the finish sprite is offscreen.

```
if (finish.getGlobalPosition().x > 256) {
  blocks.x -= 2;
}
```

When the finish sprite scrolls into the center of the canvas, the blocks container will stop moving. Notice that the code uses the finish sprite's global x position to test whether it's inside the area of the canvas. Because global coordinates are relative to the canvas, not the parent container, they're really useful for just these kinds of situations in which you want to find a nested sprite's position on the canvas.

Making Pixie Fly

The pixie character is an animated MovieClip sprite made by using three texture atlas frames. Each frame is one image in the pixie's wing-flapping animation. (Figure 7-10 illustrates these texture atlas frames.) Here's the code from the setup function that creates the pixie sprite.

```
let pixieFrames = [
  id["0.png"],
  id["1.png"],
  id["2.png"]
];
pixie = u.sprite(pixieFrames);
stage.addChild(pixie);
pixie.fps = 24;
pixie.position.set(232, 32);
pixie.vy = 0;
pixie.oldVy = 0;
```

Figure 7-10. *A stream of multicolored particles is emitted when the fairy flaps her wings*

You can see that the preceding code uses the custom `sprite` function from the `SpriteUtilities` library. Why? Because it makes creating sprites so easy!

The `pixie` sprite has a new property, called `oldVy`, which, as you'll see ahead, is going to help us calculate the pixie's vertical velocity.

To make the pixie move, the looping `play` function applies `-0.05` to her vertical velocity each frame, to create gravity.

```
pixie.vy += -0.05;
pixie.y -= pixie.vy;
```

The player can make her fly by tapping or clicking anywhere on the canvas. This is done by assigning a custom `tap` method to a `pointer` object, which you learned to create in this chapter. Each tap adds `1.5` to the pixie's vertical velocity, pushing her upward. Here's the code from the `setup` function that makes the `pointer` and assigns the `tap` method.

```
pointer = t.makePointer();
pointer.tap = () => {
  pixie.vy += 1.5;
};
```

Emitting Pixie Dust

The pixie emits a stream of multicolored particles while she's flapping her wings. The particles are constrained to an angle between 2.4 and 3.6 radians, so they're emitted within a cone-shaped wedge to the left of the pixie, as shown in Figure 7-10. The particle stream randomly emits pink, yellow, green, or violet particles, each of which is a separate frame on the texture atlas.

As you learned earlier in Chapter 5, Dust, the particle effects library, has a `create` method that will randomly display a frame on a sprite if that sprite contains multiple frames. To make this work, first define an array of texture atlas frames that you want to use for your particles.

```
dustFrames = [
  id["pink.png"],
  id["yellow.png"],
  id["green.png"],
  id["violet.png"]
];
```

Next, use those frames to initialize the sprite creation function that's supplied to the emitter (I've highlighted the most important bit of code), as follows:

```
//Create a new instance of Dust
d = new Dust(PIXI);

//Next, create the emitter
particleStream = d.emitter(
  300,                                  //The interval
  () => d.create(                       //The creation function
    pixie.x + 8,                        //x position
    pixie.y + pixie.height / 2,         //y position
    () => u.sprite(dustFrames),         //Particle sprite
    stage,                              //The parent container
    3,                                  //Number of particles
    0,                                  //Gravity
    true,                               //Random spacing
    2.4, 3.6,                           //Min/max angle
    18, 24,                             //Min/max size
    2, 3,                               //Min/max speed
    0.005, 0.01,                        //Min/max scale speed
    0.005, 0.01,                        //Min/max alpha speed
    0.05, 0.1                           //Min/max rotation speed
  )
);
```

You now have a particle emitter called particleStream. Just call its play method to make it start emitting particles.

```
particleStream.play();
```

Fine-Tuning the Pixi's Animation

When the pixie is going up, she flaps her wings and emits magical fairy dust. When she's going down, the dust stops and she stops flapping her wings. But how do we know whether she's flying upward or downward?

We have to find the difference in her velocity between the current frame and the previous frame. If her current velocity is greater than her previous velocity, she's going up. If it's less, and the previous velocity is greater than zero, she's doing down. The code stores the fairy's vy value from the current frame in a property called oldVy. When oldVy is accessed in the next frame, it tells you what the fairy's previous vy value was. Here's the code from the program's play function that does this:

```
//Decide whether or not the pixie should flap her wings
//If she's starting to go up, make her flap her wings and emit pixie dust
if (pixie.vy > pixie.oldVy) {
  if(!pixie.animating) {
    pixie.playAnimation();
    if (pixie.visible && !particleStream.playing) {
      particleStream.play();
    }
  }
}
//If she's staring to go down, stop flapping her wings, show the
//first frame and stop the pixie dust
if (pixie.vy < 0 && pixie.oldVy > 0) {
  if (pixie.animating) pixie.stopAnimation();
  pixie.show(0);
  if (particleStream.playing) particleStream.stop();
}

//Store the pixie's current `vy` value so we can use it
//to find out if the pixie has changed direction
//in the next frame. (You have to do this as the last step)
pixie.oldVy = pixie.vy;
```

The oldVy property will be used to calculate the difference in velocity between frames when the next frame swings around. This is a very well-worn trick that you can use whenever you want to compare a sprite's difference in velocity between two frames.

Collisions with the Blocks

When the pixie hits a block, she disappears in a puff of dust, as shown in Figure 7-11. How does that behavior work?

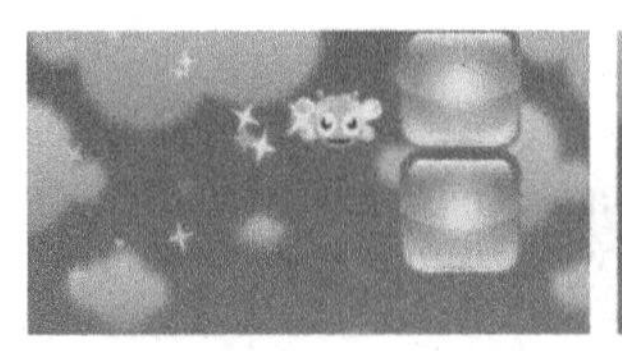
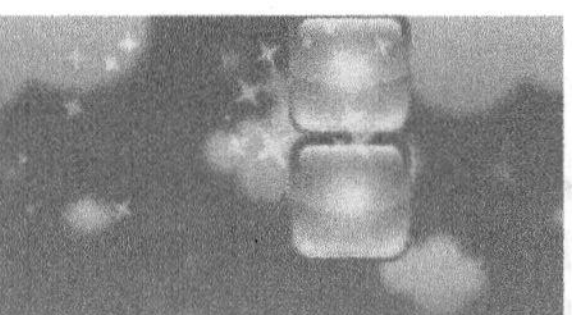
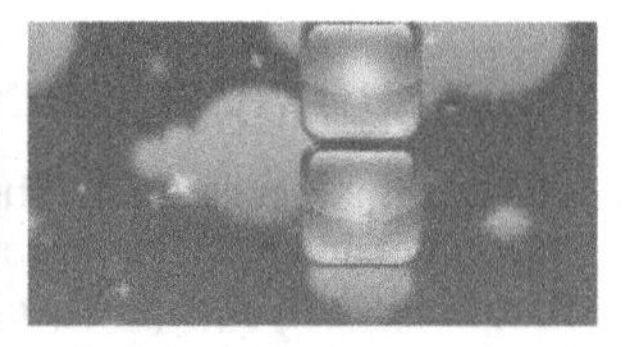

Figure 7-11. *Poof! She's gone!*

The game loop does this with the help of the Bump collision library's `hitTestRectangle` method, which you learned to use in Chapter 4. The code loops through the `blocks.children` array and tests for a collision between each block and the pixie. If `hitTestRectangle` returns `true`, the loop quits and a collision object called `pixieVsBlock` becomes `true`.

```
let pixieVsBlock = blocks.children.some(block => {
  return b.hitTestRectangle(pixie, block, true);
});
```

■ **Note** You can see that the preceding code uses JavaScript's `some` array method to loop through all the blocks. The advantage to using `some` over `forEach` is that the loop will quit as soon as it finds a value that equals `true`. That saves you from redundant additional checking.

`hitTestRectangle`'s third argument has to be `true`, so that the collision detection is done using the sprite's global coordinates. That's because the `pixie` sprite is a child of `stage`, but each `block` is a child of the `blocks` group. That means they don't share the same local coordinate space. Using their global coordinates forces `hitTestRectangle` to use the sprites' positions relative to the canvas.

If `pixieVsBlock` is `true`, and the pixie is currently visible, the collision code runs. It makes the pixie invisible, creates the particle explosion, and calls the game's `reset` function after a delay of three seconds. Here's the code from the `play` function that does this:

```
if (pixieVsBlock && pixie.visible) {

  //Make the pixie invisible
  pixie.visible = false;

  //Create a pixie dust explosion
  d.create(
    pixie.centerX, pixie.centerY, //x and y position
    () => u.sprite(dustFrames),   //Particle sprite
```

```
    stage,                    //The parent container
    20,                       //Number of particles
    0,                        //Gravity
    false,                    //Random spacing
    0, 6.28,                  //Min/max angle
    16, 32,                   //Min/max size
    1, 3                      //Min/max speed
  );

  //Stop the dust emitter that's trailing the pixie
  particleStream.stop();

  //Wait 3 seconds and then reset the game
  wait(3000).then(() => reset());
}
```

(You learned how to create the custom `wait` function in Chapter 6.)

Resetting the Game

If the pixie hits a block, the game is reset after a three-second delay. The game's `reset` function does this by repositioning the pixie and the blocks to their initial positions and makes the pixie visible again.

```
function reset() {
  pixie.visible = true;
  pixie.y = 32;
  particleStream.play();
  blocks.x = 0;
}
```

This is all the code you need to make the game start from the beginning again.

Taking It Further

And that's all there is to it! Between Pixie Perilousness! and Treasure Hunter (from Chapter 4), you have all the skills you need to start making any other game, no matter how complex. Just use the same structure and add as much detail as you require. Following are some features you might want to add to your games:

- Create different game scenes if you need to, using the technique described in Chapter 4.
- Add transitions between scenes, using the tweening technique described in Chapter 5.

- Use some text to display and update the player's score.
- Let players start the game by pressing a button (you learned how create a button in this chapter).

You're now well on your way in your career as a video game designer.

Your Next Steps

Wow, this book is almost finished! What did you learn? Everything you need to start making a rich variety of games and applications for desktop, mobile, and the Web. However, it's only a start. It's now up to you to take these skills and run with them. Here are some ideas for areas you might want to explore further:

- **Sound**. This book has been all about making engaging interactive graphics, but you'll surely want to add some sound effects and music to your work. Adding sounds is as easy as choosing one of the many excellent HTML5 sound libraries out there and using simple methods such as `load`, `play`, and `stop` to control sounds. I wrote a lightweight micro-library called sound.js (`github.com/kittykatattack/sound.js`), which has everything you need to load and play sound files, as well as generate synthesized sounds from scratch. You'll find all the instructions on how to use sound.js at its code repository; it's as easy to use as any of the other helper libraries you've used in this book. For more complex sound libraries with extra features, try Howler (`github.com/goldfire/howler.js`), Buzz (`github.com/jaysalvat/buzz`), WAD (`github.com/rserota/wad`), or the delightfully titled Theresa's Sound World (`theresassoundworld.com`).
- **Making games**. Do you want to delve deeper into game design? Then pick up a copy of this book's companion: *Advanced Game Design with HTML5 and JavaScript* (Apress, 2015). It's a comprehensive reference containing all the essential skills every game designer should know, and it's completely compatible with this book. It even shows you how to build your own rendering engine, similar to Pixi, from scratch. But, if you want to use Pixi as your rendering engine, just skip all the stuff about how to make and display sprites, and just apply the higher level functions and methodologies to what you already know about using Pixi. If you're new to game design and feel you might need to start with something more basic, pick up a copy of my *Foundation Game Design with HTML5 and JavaScript* (Apress, 2012). It's a total beginner's guide to programming and game design, and the techniques you'll learn in that book are completely compatible with the skills you've learned in this one.

- **Making applications.** The beauty of HTML5 applications is that they're completely cross-platform. You can use the same code base for the Web, mobile applications, and desktop applications. But how? The Web is easy: just dump your HTML and JS files on a web server connected to the Internet and you're done! For mobile and desktop applications, you'll require the help of a high-level wrapper. There are many to choose from, and they're easy to use. For mobile, try Cocoon (`www.ludei.com/cocoonjs`) or PhoneGap (`phonegap.com`). For desktop, try NWJS (`github.com/nwjs/nw.js`), Electron (`github.com/atom/electron`), or Adobe Air (`www.adobe.com/ca/products/air.html`). Just follow the instructions specific to each wrapper, and you'll end up with applications files that will run anywhere, on anything. Yay, HTML5!
- **Game and application development engines.** At it's heart, Pixi is just a really fast and helpful 2D image renderer. In this book you've learned how to use other helpful libraries like Bump and Charm to add features that make working with Pixi faster and easier. To make things even easier still, you can use a game engine that wraps Pixi up with a whole bunch of other useful tools and libraries to give you a fully integrated game or application development environment. I wrote a library called Hexi (`github.com/kittykatattack/hexi`) which does this just that, and is all you need to make most kinds of 2D games. It's based on exactly the same API and application architecture model you've been using in this book. Other libraries, like the popular Phaser game engine (phaser.io), also integrate Pixi with sound, physics and collision libraries. There are many helpful development tools like this out there—just choose the one that best suites your coding style.

But this is all just technology—lifeless tools! It's up to you to add the heart, soul, and imagination to bring your ideas to life. But don't take my word for it; prove it yourself. Close this book and start making some great stuff!

APPENDIX

Pixie Perilousness!—Complete Code

For your reference, here's the complete code listing for the book's final sample game: Pixie Perilousness!

The HTML Code

Following is the HTML container code that loads the main pixiePerilousness.js game file, along with the supporting helper libraries:

```
<!doctype html>
<meta charset="utf-8">
<title>Pixie Perilousness!</title>
<body>
<script src="../library/plugins/pixi.js/bin/pixi.js"></script>
<script src="../library/tink/bin/tink.js"></script>
<script src="../library/PixiDust/bin/dust.js"></script>
<script src="../library/scaleToWindow/scaleToWindow.js"></script>
<script src="../library/spriteUtilities/bin/spriteUtilities.js"></script>
<script src="../library/bump/bin/bump.js"></script>
<script src="es6/pixiePerilousness.js"></script>
</body>
```

Loading JS scripts such as this using `<script>` tags is the good old "cave man style" of loading script modules. I've done this just for simplicity, and it's a perfectly fine way to modularize your code. But, if you prefer, you could alternatively load all these files using ES6 modules, SystemJS, CommonJS, or AMD module systems.

The JavaScript Code

Here's the entire pixiePerilousness.js file code listing:

```
//Aliases
let Container = PIXI.Container,
  autoDetectRenderer = PIXI.autoDetectRenderer,
  Graphics = PIXI.Graphics,
  Sprite = PIXI.Sprite,
  MovieClip = PIXI.extras.MovieClip,
  TilingSprite = PIXI.extras.TilingSprite,
  loader = PIXI.loader,
  resources = PIXI.loader.resources,
  Text = PIXI.Text;

//Create a Pixi stage and renderer
let stage = new Container(),
    renderer = autoDetectRenderer(910, 512);
document.body.appendChild(renderer.view);

//Scale the canvas to the maximum window size
let scale = scaleToWindow(renderer.view);

//Set the initial game state
let state = play;

//load resources
loader
  .add("images/pixiePerilousness.json")
  .load(setup);

//Define any variables that might be used in more than one function
let t, b, d, pd, u, id, pointer, circle, pixie, sky, blocks,
    finish, particleStream, dustFrames;

function setup() {

  /* Initialize all the helper libraries */

  //Create a new instance of Tink, the interactive module.
  //The last argument, `scale` is
  //the return value of the `scaleToWindow` function above
  t = new Tink(PIXI, renderer.view, scale);

  //Create a new instance of Bump, the collision module
  b = new Bump(PIXI);
```

```
//Create a new instance of SpriteUtilities, for easy sprite creation
u = new SpriteUtilities(PIXI);

//Get a reference to the texture atlas frame ids
id = resources["images/pixiePerilousness.json"].textures;

/* Create the sprites */

//Make the sky background
sky = new TilingSprite(
  id["clouds.png"],
  renderer.view.width,
  renderer.view.height
);
stage.addChild(sky);

//Make the world
//Create a `Container` for all the blocks
blocks = new Container();
stage.addChild(blocks);

//What should the initial size of the gap be between the pillars?
let gapSize = 4;

//How many pillars?
let numberOfPillars = 15;

//Loop 15 times to make 15 pillars
for (let i = 0; i < numberOfPillars; i++) {

  //Randomly place the gap somewhere inside the pillar
  let startGapNumber = randomInt(0, 8 - gapSize);

  //Reduce the `gapSize` by one after every fifth pillar. This is
  //what makes gaps gradually become narrower
  if (i > 0 && i % 5 === 0) gapSize -= 1;

  //Create a block if it's not within the range of numbers
  //occupied by the gap
  for (let j = 0; j < 8; j++) {
    if (j< startGapNumber || j > startGapNumber + gapSize - 1) {
      let block = u.sprite(id["greenBlock.png"]);
      blocks.addChild(block);
```

```
      //Space each pillar 384 pixels apart. The first pillar will be
      //placed at an x position of 512
      block.x = (i * 384) + 512;
      block.y = j * 64;
    }
  }

  //After the pillars have been created, add the finish image
  //right at the end
  if (i === numberOfPillars - 1) {
    finish = u.sprite(id["finish.png"]);
    blocks.addChild(finish);
    finish.x = (i * 384) + 896;
    finish.y = 192;
  }
}

//Make the pixie sprite
let pixieFrames = [
  id["0.png"],
  id["1.png"],
  id["2.png"]
];
pixie = u.sprite(pixieFrames);
stage.addChild(pixie);
pixie.fps = 24;
pixie.position.set(232, 32);
pixie.vy = 0;
pixie.oldVy = 0;

//Create the frames array for the pixie dust images
//that trail the pixie
dustFrames = [
  id["pink.png"],
  id["yellow.png"],
  id["green.png"],
  id["violet.png"]
];

//Create the particle emitter.
//First create a new instance of Dust, the particle effects library
d = new Dust(PIXI);
```

```
  //Next, create the emitter
  particleStream = d.emitter(
    300,                                  //The interval
    () => d.create(                       //The function
      pixie.x + 8,                        //x position
      pixie.y + pixie.height / 2,         //y position
      () => u.sprite(dustFrames),         //Particle sprite
      stage,                              //The parent container
      3,                                  //Number of particles
      0,                                  //Gravity
      true,                               //Random spacing
      2.4, 3.6,                           //Min/max angle
      18, 24,                             //Min/max size
      2, 3,                               //Min/max speed
      0.005, 0.01,                        //Min/max scale speed
      0.005, 0.01,                        //Min/max alpha speed
      0.05, 0.1                           //Min/max rotation speed
    )
  );

  //Make the particle stream start playing when the game starts
  particleStream.play();

  //Make the pointer and increase the pixie's vertical
  //velocity when it's tapped
  pointer = t.makePointer();
  pointer.tap = () => {
    pixie.vy += 1.5;
  };

  //Start the game loop
  gameLoop();
}

function gameLoop(){

  //Loop this function 60 times per second
  requestAnimationFrame(gameLoop);

  //Run the current state
  state();

  //Update Tink
  t.update();

  //Update Dust
  d.update();
```

```
  //Render the stage
  renderer.render(stage);
}

function play() {

  //Make the sky background scroll by shifting the `tilePosition.x`
  //of the `sky` tiling sprite
  sky.tilePosition.x -= 1;

  //Move the blocks 2 pixels to the left each frame.
  //This will just happen while the finish image is off-screen.
  //As soon as the finish image scrolls into view, the blocks
  //container will stop moving
  if (finish.getGlobalPosition().x > 256) {
    blocks.x -= 2;
  }

  //Add gravity to the pixie
  pixie.vy += -0.05;
  pixie.y -= pixie.vy;

  //Decide whether or not the pixie should flap her wings
  //If she's starting to go up, make her flap her wings and emit pixie dust
  if (pixie.vy > pixie.oldVy) {
    if(!pixie.animating) {
      pixie.playAnimation();
      if (pixie.visible && !particleStream.playing) {
        particleStream.play();
      }
    }
  }

  //If she's staring to go down, stop flapping her wings,
  //show the first frame and stop the pixie dust
  if (pixie.vy < 0 && pixie.oldVy > 0) {
    if (pixie.animating) pixie.stopAnimation();
    pixie.show(0);
    if (particleStream.playing) particleStream.stop();
  }

  //Store the pixie's current vy so we can use it
  //to find out if the pixie has changed direction
  //in the next frame. (You have to do this as the last step)
  pixie.oldVy = pixie.vy;
```

```
//Keep the pixie contained inside the stage and
//neutralize her velocity if she hits the top or bottom boundary
let pixieVsCanvas = b.contain(
  pixie,
  {
    x: 0,
    y: 0,
    width: renderer.view.width,
    height: renderer.view.height
  }
);
if (pixieVsCanvas) {
  if (pixieVsCanvas.has("bottom") || pixieVsCanvas.has("top")) {
    pixie.vy = 0;
  }
}

//Loop through all the blocks and check for a collision between
//each block and the pixie. (`some` will quit the loop as soon as
//`hitTestRectangle` returns `true`).
//Set `hitTestRectangle`s third argument
//to `true` to use the sprites' global coordinates

let pixieVsBlock = blocks.children.some(block => {
  return b.hitTestRectangle(pixie, block, true);
});

//If there's a collision and the pixie is currently visible,
//create the explosion effect and reset the game after
//a three second delay

if (pixieVsBlock && pixie.visible) {

  //Make the pixie invisible
  pixie.visible = false;

  //Create a pixie dust explosion
  d.create(
    pixie.centerX, pixie.centerY, //x and y position
    () => u.sprite(dustFrames),   //Particle sprite
    stage,                        //The parent container
    20,                           //Number of particles
    0,                            //Gravity
    false,                        //Random spacing
    0, 6.28,                      //Min/max angle
    16, 32,                       //Min/max size
    1, 3                          //Min/max speed
  );
```

```
    //Stop the dust emitter that's trailing the pixie
    particleStream.stop();

    //Wait 3 seconds and then reset the game
    wait(3000).then(() => reset());
  }
}

//The `reset` function runs if the pixie hits a block
function reset() {

  //Reset the game if the pixie hits a block
  pixie.visible = true;
  pixie.y = 32;
  particleStream.play();
  blocks.x = 0;
}

//Helper functions

//The `randomInt` helper function
function randomInt(min, max) {
  return Math.floor(Math.random() * (max - min + 1)) + min;
}

//The `wait` helper function
function wait(duration = 0) {
  return new Promise((resolve, reject) => {
    setTimeout(resolve, duration);
  });

}
```

Index

A

B

C

D, E

F

G, H

I, J

K

L

M, N, O

P

Q

R

S

T, U

V

W, X, Y, Z

Apress®
THE EXPERT'S VOICE™

Printed in the United States
By Bookmasters